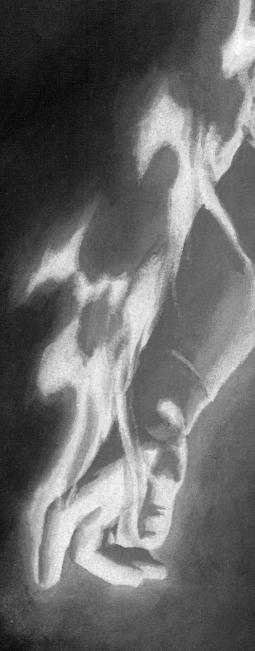

"IT IS WITH
CONSIDERABLE
DIFFICULTY THAT
I REMEMBER THE
ORIGINAL ERA OF
MY BEING..."
– *Mary Shelley*
Frankenstein

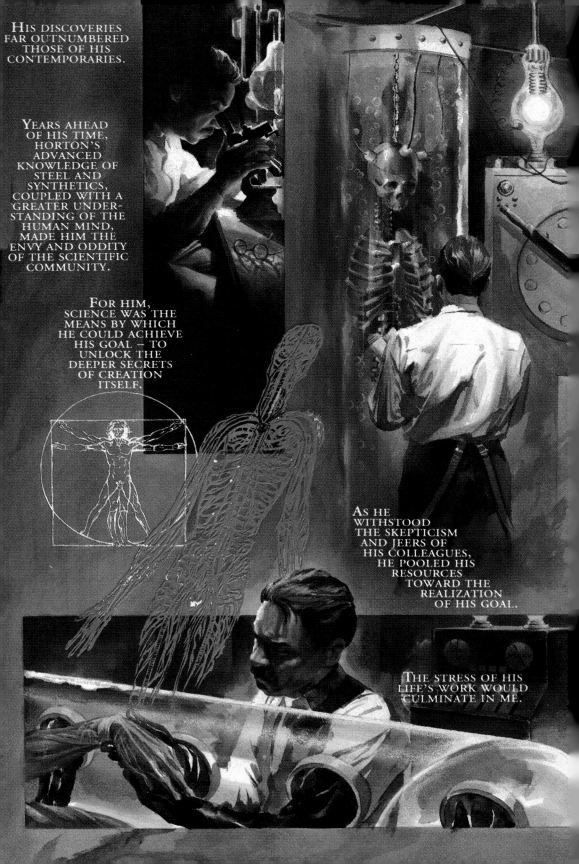

HIS DISCOVERIES FAR OUTNUMBERED THOSE OF HIS CONTEMPORARIES.

YEARS AHEAD OF HIS TIME, HORTON'S ADVANCED KNOWLEDGE OF STEEL AND SYNTHETICS, COUPLED WITH A GREATER UNDER-STANDING OF THE HUMAN MIND, MADE HIM THE ENVY AND ODDITY OF THE SCIENTIFIC COMMUNITY.

FOR HIM, SCIENCE WAS THE MEANS BY WHICH HE COULD ACHIEVE HIS GOAL — TO UNLOCK THE DEEPER SECRETS OF CREATION ITSELF.

AS HE WITHSTOOD THE SKEPTICISM AND JEERS OF HIS COLLEAGUES, HE POOLED HIS RESOURCES TOWARD THE REALIZATION OF HIS GOAL.

THE STRESS OF HIS LIFE'S WORK WOULD CULMINATE IN ME.

I CANNOT RECALL
IT PERFECTLY,
BUT IN MY FIRST
MOMENT OF
CONSCIOUSNESS,
SOMETHING
UNPREDICTED

OCCURRED.

DUE TO SOME FLAW
IN MY ORIGINAL
CONCEPTION, MY
BODY HAD AN
INCENDIARY
REACTION TO THE
CONTACT WITH
AIR.

DESPITE THIS, I REMAINED COMPLETELY UNHARMED, AND ONCE THE SUPPLY OF OXYGEN WAS CUT OFF...

...THE DESTRUCTIVE EFFECT CEASED, AND I RETURNED TO MY FORMER INERT STATE.

THE FIRST OF THOSE TO SEE ME WERE TERRIFIED BY MY PECULIAR ABILITY.

PHINEAS HORTON WAS LIKE A MODERN DAY PROMETHEUS, STEALING FIRE FROM THE HEAVENS AND HANDING A HUMAN TORCH DOWN TO MAN.

HOWEVER, MANKIND WAS NOT YET READY FOR THIS GIFT, AND HORTON WAS SCORNED FOR CREATING A POTENTIAL MENACE.

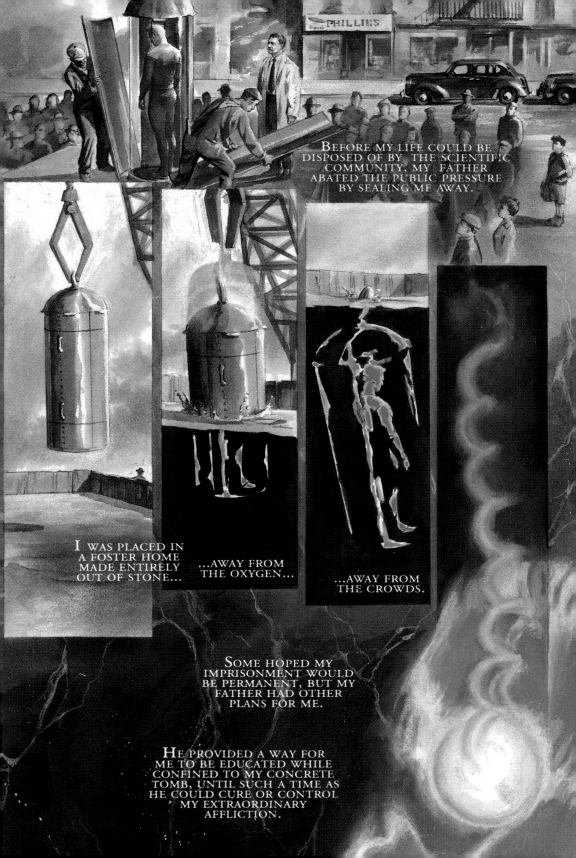

BEFORE MY LIFE COULD BE DISPOSED OF BY THE SCIENTIFIC COMMUNITY, MY FATHER ABATED THE PUBLIC PRESSURE BY SEALING ME AWAY.

I WAS PLACED IN A FOSTER HOME MADE ENTIRELY OUT OF STONE...

...AWAY FROM THE OXYGEN...

...AWAY FROM THE CROWDS.

SOME HOPED MY IMPRISONMENT WOULD BE PERMANENT, BUT MY FATHER HAD OTHER PLANS FOR ME.

HE PROVIDED A WAY FOR ME TO BE EDUCATED WHILE CONFINED TO MY CONCRETE TOMB, UNTIL SUCH A TIME AS HE COULD CURE OR CONTROL MY EXTRAORDINARY AFFLICTION.

I SPENT THIS TIME, WHICH
SEEMED LIKE YEARS, IN A
VIRTUALLY LIFELESS STATE.

I WAS TAUGHT
THE NAMES OF
OBJECTS THAT
I COULD NOT
SEE, TOUCH
OR SMELL.

I COULD ONLY
ENVISION THEM, AND
WITH NO FRAME OF
REFERENCE, IT WAS
NEXT TO IMPOSSIBLE
FROM THE VERY
BEGINNING.

I WAS LEARNING
A GREAT DEAL
ABOUT THE WORLD,
AND EVEN MORE
ABOUT THE PAIN OF
A FORCED SOLITUDE.

I WAS AWARE OF
EVERYTHING...

...UNDERSTANDING
NOTHING.

I COULD BARELY COMPREHEND
WHAT HAD HAPPENED TO ME IN
THE COURSE OF MY SHORT LIFE.

I HAD BEEN RIPPED FROM MY
ORIGINAL WOMB AND THRUST
INTO A WORLD WHERE EVERY
NOISE WAS EQUAL TO A SCREAM.

I HAD GONE FROM THE
SECURITY OF DARKNESS
TO A PLACE WHERE LIGHT
BLAZED FROM EVERY
DIRECTION.

AND YET,
AS I BECAME
AWARE OF THESE
SENSATIONS...

...AS MY EYES, .
MY EARS, AND MY
SKIN WOULD FOCUS
UPON THESE...

...THEY
DISAPPEARED.

AND I ONCE
AGAIN WOULD
FALL BACK INTO
THE DARKNESS AND
SILENCE WHICH
LACKED THE
COMFORT THEY
ONCE HELD.

THEY WERE NOW
ONLY MOCKING
REMINDERS OF ALL
THAT WAS DENIED ME.

MY FATHER BROUGHT ME
INTO THIS WORLD AND KEPT
ME ALIVE WHEN OTHERS
WOULD HAVE ME DESTROYED.

WHY, THEN, DID HE ALLOW
ME THIS TORMENT? WAS HE
SO EASILY WILLING TO
FORSAKE ME?

WAS IT POSSIBLE THAT,
WHILE I BELIEVED IN HIM
AS A FATHER...

...HE DID NOT BELIEVE IN
ME AS A SON?

I KNEW THE
AIR THAT I
HAD ONCE
TASTED.

I KNEW I
WANTED TO
TASTE IT
AGAIN,
ALWAYS AND
FOREVER.

MORE THAN
ANYTHING
ELSE,
HOWEVER, I
WANTED TO
BE WITH YOU.
I WANTED TO
BE A PART OF
YOUR WORLD.

AS MY YOUNG
MIND
DEVELOPED, I
LEARNED TO
RECOGNIZE
THE BEAUTY
AND THE
VALUE OF
HUMAN LIFE.

LIFE AND
FREEDOM
COMMANDED
MY RESPECT,
AS I POSSESSED
NEITHER.

AT THE SAME
TIME, I WAS
BECOMING
AWARE OF
MYSELF AS AN
INDIVIDUAL...

...I WAS THE
FIRST OF MY
KIND.

WAS IT RIGHT
THAT I
SHOULD BE
GIVEN LIFE,
ONLY TO BE
PLACED IN
ETERNAL IM-
PRISONMENT?

TO BE
TANTALIZED
WITH
KNOWLEDGE
OF THE
WORLD, AND
DENIED THE
CHANCE TO
SAVOR IT?

SALVATION FINALLY CAME. A TINY CRACK IN MY CONCRETE SURROUNDINGS BROUGHT IN THE SWEET AIR THAT I HAD CRAVED FOR SO LONG.

IN ONE ABRUPT MOMENT, A CATACLYSMIC BURST OF COLOR, LIGHT AND SOUND —

I WAS FREE.
AS AT THE MOMENT OF MY BIRTH.
I SCREAMED.
I WAS FINALLY FREE TO BREATHE AGAIN — TO FEEL THE RUSH OF HEAT ANIMATE MY FRAME.

MY FATHER TRIED TO CALL ME BACK...

...BUT KNOWING WHAT HE HAD DENIED ME, I RAN...

...AFRAID OF BEING IMPRISONED AGAIN.

I RAN BLINDLY INTO THE NIGHT, AND EXPERIENCED AGAIN THE PANIC AND ASTONISHMENT THAT MY MENACING APPEARANCE PROVOKED IN PEOPLE.

I HAVE SINCE LEARNED TO CONTROL MY CONDITION...

...AND HAVE COME TO MEAN SOMETHING VERY DIFFERENT TO THIS SOCIETY IN WHICH I NOW BELONG.

AS I HAVE LEARNED SINCE, I WAS NOT THE FIRST ANOMALY TO EXIST...

...BUT ON THAT DAY OF MY FREEDOM IN 1939, THIS WORLD HAD ITS FIRST CONFRONTAION WITH THE FANTASTIC.

THE GOLDEN AGE OF MIRACLES WOULD BEGIN, AND IN THE YEARS TO COME, THE WORLD WOULD KNOW THE PRESENCE OF THE UNNATURAL AND EXTRAORDINARY AS PART OF REALITY.

Credits

Kurt Busiek
Writer

Alex Ross
Artist/Cover Design

**Richard Starkings/
Comicraft**
Lettering & Interior Design

Joe Kaufman
Logo Design

Marc McLaurin
Editor

Spencer Lamm
Assistant Editor

Tom DeFalco
Editor in Chief

Foreword **Stan Lee**

Commentaries **Kurt Busiek**

Alex Ross

John Romita Sr.

Afterword **Scott McCloud**

Foreword by
Stan Lee

It's unbelievable!

I was actually *asked* to write this foreword! As if I'd say no! As if I wouldn't have *fought* for the chance! As if I'd have let *anyone* else write the foreword to a series that I consider the most innovative, brilliantly conceived and skillfully executed concept to come along in years!

MARVELS is far more than just another comic book title. In fact, referring to it as merely a comic book would be like referring to World War Two as a disturbing little fracas. Artwise, scriptwise and formatwise, MARVELS is a giant leap forward, bringing us to a new plateau in the evolution of illustrated literature.

In case I'm not making myself clear, I think it's pretty cool.

You know, creating the Marvel Universe was considered to be somewhat daring and revolutionary when we first structured it many years ago. Never before had one comic book company's burgeoning cast of characters, both heroic and villainous,

lived in the same world — mainly in the same city, New York — where they would meet and interface with each other just as we all do in our everyday lives. Never before had a comic book company striven so conscientiously to inject realism into its stories by using the names of real cities, real buildings, real vehicles and real events whenever possible. Thus, the Marvel Universe was born. But, never before, not until Kurt Busiek and Alex Ross created MARVELS, had that universe seemed quite so undeniably authentic, so unquestionably credible, so eminently compelling.

Of all the countless graphic novels published during the last few decades, novels masterfully scripted and magnificently illustrated, none have brought the reader directly into the story the way MARVELS does, none have made the reader a part of the events that transpired the way MARVELS does, and none have made the reader feel as though he or she is on the scene, witnessing history in the making the way MARVELS does.

I'm sure you can readily understand my unbounded enthusiasm for these wonderfully rendered tales. You see, I was there at the beginning. I was lucky enough to have worked with such towering talents as Carl Burgos, creator of the Human Torch, and with Bill Everett who brought us the Sub-Mariner, as well as with Syd Shores, Al Avison, Joe Maneely, and all the other shining stars of the forties and fifties. No, I haven't forgotten the great Jack Kirby. He deserves a very special mention. Even in those early days, those glorious days when he, together with Joe Simon, brought us Captain America, he was in a class by himself, just as he was for the next half-century when we worked together on THE FANTASTIC FOUR, THE INCREDIBLE HULK, THE UNCANNY X-MEN and so many other titles that are still among the world's best-selling comic books. Then, of course, there was the amazing Steve Ditko, who breathed life into

Spider-Man and Doctor Strange, whose unique genius helped to make those characters the unforgettable, legendary icons they are today.

Indeed, all the colorful, costumed cavorters depicted in this fabulous volume of **MARVELS** owe their enduring popularity to so many wonderful comic book superstars whose lives have touched yours and mine throughout the years, people like John Romita, John Buscema, Gene Colan, Joe Sinnott, Don Heck, John Severin, Wally Wood, Gil Kane, Dick Ayers, Larry Lieber, Marie Severin, Roy Thomas, Chris Claremont, John Byrne, Ross Andru — the list goes on endlessly.

That's why this book means so much to me. Kurt and Alex have taken characters who are the foundation of Marvel Comics, characters who have been part of my life, and possibly yours, for decades, characters on whom all the people mentioned above have lavished so much time, effort and enthusiasm for so many years, and they have presented them in a manner never seen before, a style breathtaking new and astonishingly realistic.

The absorbing chronicle you're about to read features virtually every one of Marvel Comics' major super heroes, as well as a number of vile and vicious villains who have become part of the fabric of comicdom's lore. And yet, perhaps for the first time in magazine history, these are not merely the adventures of the heroes and villains, but rather the adventures and logical reactions of the ordinary citizens whose lives are impacted by our super characters. In fact, the true hero of the **MARVELS** saga is a distinctly non-superpowered photojournalist through whose eyes the entire epic unfolds. Though the pages are filled with action and spectacle, the scenes are far different from those you'll see in any comic book, the emphasis is different, the tone is different, the approach is different. Kurt Busiek and Alex Ross have achieved a rare literary and artistic triumph by maintaining ever-mounting suspense and excitement without any of the usual life-and-death battles continuing for page after page, which you'll find in the average comic book. I've never read anything like the stories on the pages ahead, nor have I ever seen anything surpassing the spectacular artwork

which brings each episode so glowingly to life, and I'm sure, after you've read them, you'll enthusiastically echo those sentiments.

In closing, I feel I can speak for all the artists and writers whose work is so gloriously honored on the pages of **MARVELS** when I say that these tales are a glowing tribute to what has gone before, and an inspiring presage of what is yet to come. They have taken comics to the next level of entertainment by adding a dimension and a reality that has seldom, *if ever,* been seen in the medium. I've read these stories over and over, each time finding something new and surprising. Having them all together in one volume is the ultimate luxury, as well as the ultimate proof that tales told in illustrated format can favorably compete with *any* and *every* form of literature.

Excelsior!

STAN LEE

Chapter One

A TIME OF MARVELS

-- AND YOU'LL SEE --

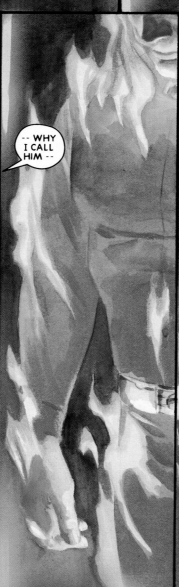

-- WHY I CALL HIM --

G-GOOD LORD!

The HUMAN TORCH!

THE SUDDEN JOLT OF *SHOCK* AND *TERROR* ROCKED US BACK LIKE A PHYSICAL BLOW. BUT IT ONLY LASTED A MOMENT.

THEN COMMON SENSE REASSERTED ITSELF. THE THING WAS A FAKE -- IT *HAD* TO BE!

-- AND *FRIGHTENED PEOPLE* WHO FELT SAFE A MINUTE OR TWO AGO, TRYING TO GET OUT OF THE WAY BUT NOT SURE WHICH WAY TO *RUN.*

I'VE GOTTA GET TO A *PHONE...*

WE BARELY EVEN SAW ANY OF THE *ACTION,* IT MOVED SO FAST...

LOOK! THERE HE *GOES!*

I'M NO FAN OF THAT GUY -- I DON'T HOLD WITH PEOPLE *BUILT FROM A KIT* --

BUT RIGHT HERE AN' NOW, I HOPE HE GIVES THAT WATER-BREATHING JERK *WHAT FOR!*

DON'T SAY THAT! YOU DON'T KNOW WHAT YOU'RE *TALKING ABOUT!*

Huh?

AND YOU ARE -- ?

BETTY DEAN, POLICEWOMAN. I'VE *MET* NAMOR -- HE'S ONLY TRYING TO GET WHAT HE CONSIDERS JUSTICE FOR HIS PEOPLE! YOU SHOULDN'T JUDGE HIM UNTIL YOU KNOW *BOTH SIDES* OF THE STORY!

"PEOPLE?" THERE'S MORE THAN *ONE* OF HIM?

HEY! DIDJA *HEAR?* THAT SUB-MARINER GUY JUST FLOODED THE HOLLAND TUNNEL -- AN' *IT'S FULLA CARS!*

I'VE *GOT* TO GET TO A PHONE...

YOU'LL HAVE TO *EXCUSE* US, OFFICER DEAN --

-- MUCH AS WE'D LOVE TO LISTEN TO YOU MAKE EXCUSES FOR A *RAMPAGING MANIAC* -- WE HAVE *WORK* TO DO.

WE DIDN'T CATCH UP TO EITHER OF THEM AT THE TUNNEL -- *OR* THE CENTRAL PARK ZOO -- *OR* THE GEORGE WASHINGTON BRIDGE.

IT WASN'T UNTIL THEY REACHED THE STATUE OF LIBERTY THAT WE GOT MORE THAN A GLIMPSE OF THEM --

SEE -- *THERE!* UP ON THE *STATUE!*

-- AND AT THAT, IT WAS FROM QUITE A DISTANCE...

THE SUB-MARINER'S BLOWN OUT THE TORCH'S *FIRE* SOMEHOW -- AND HE'S *THROWIN'* HIM OFF!

WE HELD OUR BREATH AS THE TORCH BURST INTO FLAME AGAIN --

-- BUT --

TOO LATE - HE HIT THE DRINK! AND LOOK! THAT *FISH-FACED RAT'S* DIVIN' IN *AFTER* HIM!

SAY, CAN ROBOTS *DROWN?*

THE TORCH'S ESCAPE, SOME MINUTES LATER, WAS HIDDEN FROM US BY A COAL BARGE, SO WE MISSED THAT TOO --

-- BUT AT LEAST I FINALLY REACHED A PHONE...

YOU'RE **ALL RIGHT**, DORIS? NOTHING'S --

NO -- THERE WAS SOME NOISE AND THE BUILDING SHOOK, BUT THAT'S ALL.

IT'S **YOU** I'M WORRIED ABOUT -- OUT THERE IN ALL THAT --

LOOK -- GET TO **LANIGAN'S** AND WAIT FOR ME THERE. THERE'LL BE NEWSMEN THERE -- SO IF ANYTHING HAPPENS, YOU'LL KNOW RIGHT AWAY.

AND THE BUILDING'S **SOLID AS A ROCK** --!

PHIL! KISS'ER FOR ME AND HANG UP! WE'RE GOIN' TO **RADIO CITY**!

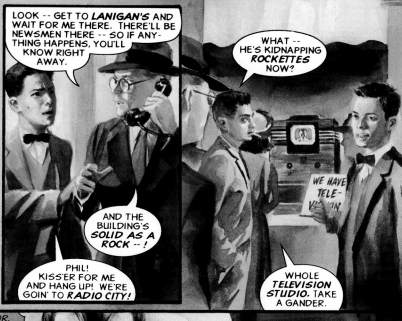

WHAT -- HE'S KIDNAPPING **ROCKETTES** NOW?

WE HAVE TELE-VISION

WHOLE **TELEVISION STUDIO**. TAKE A GANDER.

THIS IS PRINCE NAMOR, THE SUB-MARINER -- WITH A MESSAGE FOR THE SO-CALLED **HUMAN TORCH**!

THIS IS MY **FINAL WARNING!** GET OFF MY TRAIL, TORCH --

-- OR SUFFER THE CONSEQUENCES!

OF COURSE, ALL WE FOUND AT RADIO CITY WAS SCARED EMPLOYEES, WRECKED EQUIPMENT AND HOLES IN THE WALLS.

THE TORCH AND THE SUB-MARINER HAD HOT-FOOTED IT UPSTATE, AND THE ROADS WERE TOO JAMMED WITH PANICKED NEW YORKERS TO FOLLOW --

SO WHILE THEY **WHEELED** AND **SOARED** AND **CLASHED** IN THE SPRING SUNSHINE --

-- WE KEPT TO THE SHADOWS AND STRAINED FOR **ANY WORD** OF THEM.

CAN'T YOU GET ANY BETTER RECEPTION THAN **THAT**, LANIGAN?

SHH!

-- REPEAT THE **LATEST DEVELOPMENTS:** THE HUMAN TORCH HAD IMPRISONED THE SUB-MARINER BENEATH A **SHEET OF FLAME** IN AN UPSTATE RESERVOIR --

-- BUT THE **UNDERSEA DYNAMO** FREED HIMSELF -- EVEN AS THE ARMY **BOMBED** HIS FIERY PRISON!

WE WILL CONTINUE TO BRING YOU UPDATES AS THEY OCCUR, BUT NOW A WORD FROM --

BLAST THEM!

WHAT IS IT, PHIL? WHAT'S WRONG?

LOOK AT US -- JUST **SITTING HERE,** WAITING! THERE ISN'T A **THING** WE CAN DO --

-- AND THIS IS **OUR** CITY! **OUR WORLD!**

WHO GAVE **THEM** THE RIGHT TO JUST COME IN AND **TAKE IT AWAY** FROM US?!

LOOK **ALIVE**, KIDS! POLICE POOL SAYS THE TORCH IS BACK IN TOWN -- AND HEADED FOR THE **TORPEY CHEMICAL WORKS!**

HE'S UP TO SOMETHING, ALL RIGHT!

LET'S **MOVE!**

AS LUCK WOULD HAVE IT, THE POLICE HAD CLEARED THE BRIDGES BY THEN. AND OUR **PRESS CREDENTIALS** GOT US THROUGH...

BOY, PHIL -- I'VE GOT TO HAND IT TO YOU. YOU'RE ONE **SMART GUY!**

Huh?

IF YOU'D TAKEN THAT JOB, YOU'D BE ON A STEAMER TO EUROPE RIGHT NOW -- AN' YOU'D BE **MISSIN' THIS!**

WHO CARES ABOUT THE WAR IN EUROPE ANY-MORE? WE GOT OUR OWN WAR **RIGHT HERE --**

-- AND THIS TIME **WE'RE** JOHNNY-ON-THE-SPOT!

IT WAS THE FIRST THING I HEARD IN ALL THIS THAT MADE ANY SENSE.

IT **WAS** LIKE A WAR -- NOT JUST THE BATTLES, BUT THE VERY FACT OF THE MARVELS THEM-SELVES. A WAR -- OR SOME **FREAKISH, VIOLENT STORM.**

AND ALL WE COULD DO -- ALL ANYONE COULD DO -- WAS HOLD FAST AND HOPE TO **RIDE IT OUT.**

IT'S THAT COP -- THAT **DEAN** WOMAN! SHE'S GOTTEN 'EM TO MAKE NICE AT EACH OTHER! I DON'T **BELIEVE** IT!

THEY'RE ACTUALLY **SMILIN'** AT EACH OTHER!

IF THEY SHAKE HANDS, I'M **DEFINITELY** GONNA THROW UP!

PHIL -- WHAT ARE YOU SAYING?

I DON'T WANT A SUPERMAN, DARLING. I JUST --

YOU DON'T UNDERSTAND. A MAN --

MAYBE -- WE SHOULD PUT OUR WEDDING PLANS OFF FOR A LITTLE WHILE. JUST --

-- JUST UNTIL THIS IS ALL OVER.

-- A MAN'S GOT TO BE ABLE TO PROTECT HIS FAMILY. IF HE CAN'T DO THAT --

-- HE'S GOT NO BUSINESS BEING A HUSBAND.

IF THAT'S HOW YOU FEEL, PHIL --

-- YOU'D BETTER HAVE THIS BACK. I WOULDN'T WANT TO BURDEN YOU.

DORIS -- I --

IF YOU EVER WANT TO GIVE IT BACK, YOU KNOW WHERE TO FIND ME.

WHEN THIS IS OVER, I'D SAID. WHEN WOULD THAT BE?

IT WOULD BLOW OVER. THE WORLD WOULDN'T STAY LIKE THIS. IT COULDN'T.

COULD IT?

THIS MUST HAVE BEEN WHAT LONDONERS FELT LIKE DURING THE *BLITZ.* THEY FELT SO *SAFE*, ON THEIR SIDE OF THE CHANNEL -- AND THEN --

-- THEN THE CHANNEL DIDN'T *MEAN ANYTHING* ANYMORE.

WE LISTENED FOR *INSTRUCTIONS* -- FOR EVACUATION PLANS --

AND WE LISTENED AS THE SUB-MARINER WAS REPORTED TO BE ATTACKING IN *AFRICA* --

-- BERLIN --

-- CANADA --

AOOOGAH

ATTENTION! ATTENTION! THIS IS NOT A DRILL!

THE SUB-MARINER IS HEADED FOR NEW YORK!

THIS IS NOT A DRILL!

PLEASE PROCEED TO YOUR NEAREST SHELTER IMMEDIATELY!

AOOOGAH

PHIL -- ?

I KNEW WHAT SHE WAS THINKING.

IT WAS SOMETHING TO *SEE*.

BY THE TIME I WOKE UP, IT WAS *ALL OVER* -- IN MORE WAYS THAN ONE.

REPARATIONS WERE BEING MADE, AND THE SUB-MARINER WAS ON THE SIDE OF THE *ANGELS* AGAIN.

BUT MORE IMPORTANTLY, JAPAN HAD ATTACKED *PEARL HARBOR*, WE WERE AT WAR WITH THE AXIS POWERS, AND NOBODY HAD THE TIME TO WORRY ABOUT THE MARVELS ANYMORE.

PHIL? THEY SAID YOU WERE --

HIYA, SWEETHEART. THESE FLOWERS ALL FROM YOU?

NOPE -- THEY'RE FROM HER.

OH, PHIL!

YOUR EYE -- THE DOCTORS SAID --

Um -- HOW DO YOU -- ?

HOW DO I FEEL? YOU MEAN, ASIDE FROM WONDERING WHETHER MONOCULAR VISION WILL IMPROVE MY PHOTOGRAPHY?

AM I MAD AT THE **MARVELS** FOR TAKING MY EYE? AM I GOING TO SWEAR VENGEANCE ON THEM --

-- DEVOTE MY LIFE TO **DESTROYING THEM ALL** OR DRIVING THEM OUT OF OUR WORLD SO EVERYTHING CAN BE THE WAY IT **WAS** AGAIN?

IS THAT WHAT YOU'RE ASKING?

Um -- SOMETHING LIKE THAT.

NAH.

I'M GOING TO HAVE MORE IMPORTANT THINGS TO DO. THERE'S A **WAR ON,** FOR ONE.

AND WE'VE GOT A **WEDDING** TO PLAN -- THAT IS, IF YOU'RE WILLING TO MARRY **POPEYE THE CAMERA MAN.**

BUT -- I --

BUT --

-- BUT --

AW, SHUT UP AND **KISS ME,** WOULD YOU?

WELL, **I'D** SAY HE'S RECOVERED.

I WAS 4-F THANKS TO MY EYE, BUT I DID GET TO EUROPE -- AS THE WAR CORRESPONDENT I'D WANTED TO BE AT THE START.

the food here's lousy, but what do you expect? I think it's last year's leftovers from the Bugle lunchroom.

MOVING OUT IN A FEW MINUTES, PHIL.

I'LL BE READY, CASEY.

I've been thinking about what I tried to tell you when I left - about that day and what happened? I think I know how to say it now.

I'd been waiting for the marvels to go away - and what I realized that day - what maybe we all realized.

They weren't some temporary thing like the World's Fair or the Olympics, or even the war. They were for real.

your loving husband, Phil

End of Book One

Kurt Busiek

I never read these stories when they were first published.

Oh, maybe a few of them, here and there, slipped in among the stacks of RICHIE RICH and BATMAN in my friends' basements, or purchased furtively from the local drugstore, read hastily and then stuffed behind the big air-conditioning unit in the train station between the drugstore and my home (my parents did not allow comic books into the house), but I never read them in any organized manner, never got a sense of the Marvel Universe as a whole. And

when I did read the stories **MARVELS** is based on, it was as back issues and reprints — a run of THE UNCANNY X-MEN, or THE FANTASTIC FOUR or THE AVENGERS or THE AMAZING SPIDER-MAN or whatever. That way, I learned about the characters and their history and their troubles, but seldom learned how those individual tracks fit together, seldom got a sense of what was happening in the other books at the time each series was progressing.

So when I came to do **MARVELS** and set out to explore the world these stories take place in, rather than the individual adventures of the heroes, I had to put it all in order, chart it out and see what the breadth of the Marvel Universe held alongside the depth. I got to discover that Tony Stark was being harassed by the Senate in his own series while he was busy helping create S.H.I.E.L.D for the government over in STRANGE TALES, how quickly Hawkeye, Quicksilver and the Scarlet Witch went from villains in TALES OF SUSPENSE and UNCANNY X-MEN to heroes in AVENGERS, and more, and I got to use it, more often than not, in the stories.

And the one thing I continually discovered was this: There's no substitute for hands-on research.

I had all the fancy artistic goals. I knew my themes. I knew the grand scope of the stories I wanted to tell. But without the details, it could never have come through the way it did. Had I been able to go back in time and have things set up for me, I couldn't have asked for better. How was I to know, when I wanted to set up Galactus as an apocalyptic figure in #3, that a TALES TO ASTONISH/AVENGERS story a few months prior had religious nuts prophesying the coming end? How was I to know, when I wanted a wide-scale crisis to set the stage for the very human-scale drama of the Green Goblin's kidnapping of Gwen Stacy in #4, that the forces of Atlantis had invaded Manhattan right beforehand? How was I to know that right when I wanted to set up the contrast between the lionizing of the super heroes and the demonizing of the mutants, that over in TALES TO ASTONISH, Benson's Department Store was introducing a line of clothing inspired by the Wasp? *(Okay, so it was all a plot by The Magician to use the Wasp's vanity to ambush her, but it was there...)*

I mean, I knew the *stories*. I just didn't realize how they fit together.

And sometimes, even when I did know how the stories fit together, I didn't suspect how well. Take the climax of Book Two here, with the wedding of Reed and Sue Richards and the debut of the mutant-hunting Sentinels. I knew that the two stories had to happen reasonably close together (since the Human Torch appearance in X-MEN #13, one month before the Sentinels showed up in publishing time, mentions the upcoming wedding), and I definitely wanted to juxtapose the two events — the ultimate example of the FF as the "royalty" of the Marvel Universe and the ultimate expression of fear and hatred of the mutants — but when I went to figure out which came first, well...

Here's how it works: The wedding had to happen after the X-Men fought the Juggernaut, since that was the story the Torch guest-starred in. But the X-Men *attend* the wedding, and at the end of the Juggernaut story, the X-Men are all injured and bed-ridden — and they're still recuperating at the beginning of the Sentinels story, so it can't happen between those two issues. But they're all injured again by the end of the 3-part Sentinels story, and are hospitalized in the beginning of the next issue, which flows right into a 2-part Magneto story — and by the time *that's* over, we're 5 or 6 months beyond the wedding in publishing time. So it must happen *during* an issue, and as it turns out, the only time during that stretch that the X-Men are uninjured and otherwise unoccupied is very early in the Sentinels story — a period of less than two days.

So there I was, looking for the juxtaposition of the two events — and wouldn't you know it, the only way for them to work out is *if they happen at almost the same time*. Whatever my lofty plans for the climax of **MARVELS** #2, it had just become far more powerful, and all because of the minor details of the source material.

I kept running into this as I researched and wrote **MARVELS**. I'd need something — and *there* it was. I'd want to set up some emotional point, some thematic symbol — and *there* was the evidence for it in Marvel history, as if it had been waiting for me.

And that's the point of this piece, I guess. For all that **MARVELS** has won praise for its humanity, for its perspective, for its depiction of a complex and mostly-believable world, and for all

that I'm willing to accept credit for what I contributed to the project (and for most of what Alex contributed, when he's not around to hear), it ultimately boils down to this: If it wasn't out there in the first place, it couldn't have ended up in here.

So I owe a major debt of thanks to my uncredited collaborators — Carl Burgos, Bill Everett, Joe Simon, Jack Kirby, Stan Lee, Steve Ditko, Don Heck, Gene Colan, Dick Ayers, Roy Thomas, John Romita, Gerry Conway, John Buscema, Mike Friedrich, Gil Kane, Steve Gerber, Neal Adams, Werner Roth, Wally Wood and so many others. Thanks to one and all for creating such an involving, entertaining and multi-faceted fantasy world. It's the height of fatuousness to say we couldn't have done it without you — we wouldn't have had anywhere to start. We wouldn't have had any reason to come up with the idea in the first place.

We wouldn't even be in this line of business.

Thanks, guys. It was a rare treat to revisit the world you built.

Kurt

KURT BUSIEK

Chapter Two

MONSTERS
AMONG US

IT WASN'T THAT LONG AGO -- BUT IT WAS A DIFFERENT TIME.

LOOK ALIVE, PEOPLE!

THREE OF THOSE COSTUMED MANIACS ARE RIPPING UP DOWNTOWN! THEY GOT A MAD ON FOR THE AVENGERS AND THEY'RE TAKIN' IT OUT ON US!

ALL I WANT TO SEE ARE REAR ENDS HEADED FOR THE --

PHIL -- YOU'RE STILL HERE! GOOD.

HERE'S FIVE ROLLS OF FILM. USE 'EM UP -- I DON'T WANT THE BUGLE BEATING US OUT AGAIN.

MISTER BUSHKIN -- AS A FREELANCER, I DON'T ALLY MYSELF WITH --

DOUBLE RATE FOR EXCLUSIVE FIRST-USE -- WHAT-EVER YOU GET.

YOU GOT IT.

THERE WAS SO MUCH ENERGY IN NEW YORK, AS IF FIREWORKS HAD BEEN GOING OFF FOR MONTHS --

THE BIRTH OF THE FANTASTIC FOUR --

THOR --

GIANT-MAN --

THE RETURN OF THE SUB-MARINER --

AND OF COURSE, THE BIGGEST BLAST OF ALL -- THE SHOW-STOPPER THAT LIT UP THE WORLD LIKE A DOZEN FOURTH OF JULYS ROLLED INTO ONE --

THERE HE IS!

SO WHO DO YOU THINK WE SHOULD GET TO WRITE THE *TEXT?*

ISAAC ASIMOV?

BEN URICH?

NORMAN MAILER?

WELL, SINCE YOU MENTION IT -- I WAS KIND OF HOPING *I* COULD TAKE A CRACK AT IT...

HMMM...

THAT'D BE ALL RIGHT, I SUPPOSE -- BUT I'M NOT GOING TO GIVE YOU A CONTRACT WITHOUT SEEING SOME *SAMPLES.*

TELL YOU WHAT -- YOU COME BACK WITH A *CHAPTER* OR TWO -- OR ANYTHING THAT SHOWS ME YOU CAN *WRITE* --

-- AND IT'S A DEAL.

THANKS. YOU WON'T *REGRET* THIS.

NOT IF IT MAKES *MONEY,* I WON'T.

IT'S BEEN A *PLEASURE,* PHIL.

A BOOK.

I WAS GOING TO WRITE A *BOOK.*

HOW WOULD IT *START?*

Ⓗ ERAKLES AND GILGAMESH. Roland and King Arthur. The names of legend. But the legends are being outshone, in the form of *NAH, TOO HIGHBROW.*

EVERYBODY KNEW THAT.

THE X-MEN.

I'D NEVER SEEN THEM BEFORE, BUT I'D *HEARD* OF THEM.

-- BUT YOU NEVER COULD *TELL.*

WHAT'SA *MATTER,* GIRLIE? REAL HUMANS NOT *GOOD ENOUGH* FOR YA?

SAME TO YOU!

WE DON'T WANT YOUR KIND AROUND HERE!

THEY WERE CRIMINALS -- *KILLERS* --

STINKIN' MUTIES!

STAY *BACK!* DON'T *TOUCH ME!*

YOU HEARD THE LADY! *BACK OFF!*

SUPER-POWERED MUTANTS. *FREAKS.* THEY *LOOKED* JUST LIKE NORMAL PEOPLE --

WE MOVED IN --

THERE WAS A CHUNK OF **BRICK** IN MY HAND --

OWW!

WHY, YOU **MISERABLE** -- !

ICEMAN -- **DON'T!**

FORGET ABOUT IT! THEY'RE NOT **WORTH** IT!

LIKE A **SUMMER SQUALL**, IT ENDED QUICKLY.

THE ONE THEY CALLED **CYCLOPS** BLASTED A HOLE IN THE WALL, AND THEY VANISHED INTO THE SHADOWS.

THE CROWD **DISPERSED.**

BUT HIS **WORDS** STAYED WITH ME.

"THEY'RE NOT **WORTH** IT."

"NOT **WORTH** IT."

WHAT DID HE MEAN BY **THAT?!**

PHIL! I *THOUGHT* I HEARD YOU COME IN!

HOW WAS YOUR DAY?

PRETTY GOOD, I SOLD MY BOOK, I THINK.

THAT'S *WONDERFUL!*

SO -- WHAT ARE YOU NOT *TELLING* ME? WHY DO YOU SOUND SO *WORRIED?*

WHAT WAS I GOING TO *SAY?* THAT I WAS SCARED MUTANTS WOULD ENSLAVE OUR DAUGHTERS?

I'M -- NOT SURE JENNY AND BETH SHOULD *IDOLIZE* THE MARVELS THAT WAY, DORIS.

IT MIGHT NOT BE *HEALTHY* --

OH *TOSH.* THEY'RE HEALTHY AS TWO *MONKEYS.*

AND NEED I REMIND YOU THAT IF YOU HADN'T GOTTEN OVER YOUR *FEAR* OF THOSE GUYS --

-- WE'D NEVER HAVE GOTTEN *MARRIED.*

IT WASN'T *FEAR*, EXACTLY...

OKAY -- *I'M* GONNA BE THE HUMAN TORCH. YOU BE *THE EEL* --

ICK!

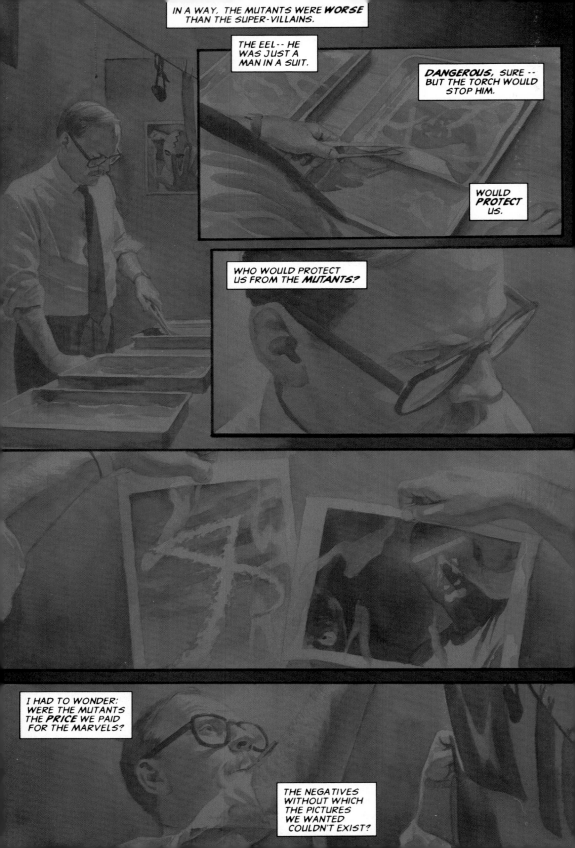

AFTER A *GOOD NIGHT'S SLEEP*, THOUGH, I PUT THE MUTANTS OUT OF MY MIND.

THINGS WERE BACK TO *NORMAL*.

WE HAVEN'T MOVED IN *TEN MINUTES*. WHAT'S THE HOLDUP?

IT'S ON THE RADIO! *GIANT-MAN'S* FIGHTING *SPIDER-MAN* -- THE POLICE HAVE *BLOCKADED* THE AREA!

TRAFFIC'S BACKED UP -- THE TERMINAL'S A *MESS*!

CAN YOU *SEE* THEM FROM HERE?

WHAT DID SPIDER-MAN *DO*?

I WAS THINKING ABOUT PUTTING A *NEW SECTION* IN MY BOOK -- JUST PICTURES OF PEOPLE *REACTING* TO THE MARVELS.

LOOK! IT'S *THOR*!

WHERE -- ?

LET ME *SEE*!

WHERE'S HE *HEADED* -- AVENGERS MANSION?

WHO *CARES*? CAN YOU *SEE* 'EM?

WHAT IF ONE OF THEM RIPPED SOMEONE'S *CAR* IN HALF? WHAT WOULD THE *OWNER* DO?

PROBABLY TRY TO GET HIM TO *AUTOGRAPH* THE PIECES.

"-- IT'S NOT A TOTAL LOSS."

LOOK! OVER *THERE!* IS THAT --?

SAY!

-- MY *AUTOGRAPH BOOK* --

REED RICHARDS AND *SUSAN STORM*, WHOSE ROMANCE WAS A-LEVEL NEWS IN ALL THE GOSSIP COLUMNS, WERE THERE.

-- STANDING RIGHT IN FRONT OF THE STATUE SHE *DID* OF HIM!

-- GONNA JUST *DIE* --

NO, I FIGURED BARNEY WAS MAKING A PRETTY *SAFE BET,* CONSIDERING THE PICTURES I WAS GETTING.

-- SUCH A *WONDERFUL COUPLE,* DON'T YOU THINK --?

OF COURSE, HE DID HAVE THE *GLOBE'S SOCIETY* MAN THERE, TOO -- AND NO WONDER.

-- HEARD THAT ON THE *SIDE,* SHE AND THE *SUB-MARINER* --

-- WELL, I *NEVER* --!

THE *HUMAN TORCH* WAS THERE, WITH SOME PRETTY TEENAGER.

C'MON, DORRIE -- LET'S GRAB SOME *PUNCH.*

AND MAYBE I'LL HEAT UP A FEW *HORS D'OEUVRES* FOR YOU...

JOHNNY STORM, DON'T YOU *DARE* --!

WE *ALL* THOUGHT THAT, BACK THEN.

JENNY, SIT UP *STRAIGHT.* BETH -- ELBOWS OFF THE TABLE.

SO DID MISTER BUSHKIN LIKE YOUR ARTICLE?

HM?

I JUST TURNED IT IN TO HIM TODAY -- HE DIDN'T HAVE A CHANCE TO READ IT WHILE I WAS THERE.

OH, BUT I STOPPED BY THE *DAILY GAZETTE* OFFICES TODAY.

THEY'RE DOING A THINK PIECE ON THE WILLIAMS *EMBEZZLEMENT* CASE -- BOUGHT A BUNCH OF MY *IRON MAN* PICTURES.

UM -- WHAT'S THE CONNEC- TION?

WILLIAMS INNOVATIONS AND STARK INDUSTRIES ARE *COMPETITORS,* HONEY.

WILLIAMS CLAIMS STARK'S THE REASON HIS COMPANY IS *FAILING.* PRETTY LUDICROUS IF YOU ASK ME.

=giggle!=

SHH!

BUT I GUESS I OWE HIM A *COMMISSION* -- I'D HARDLY HAVE SOLD THOSE PHOTOS OTHERWISE.

YOU SHUSH!

THEY WERE ACHINGLY *INNOCENT* -- AND I WANTED SO MUCH TO SHIELD THEM FROM ANYTHING THAT'D CHANGE THAT.

PLAYING THEIR *LITTLE-GIRL* GAMES -- SWIPING TABLE SCRAPS FOR SOME STRAY *DOG* OR *CAT* THEY'D BEFRIENDED --

IT WAS ONLY FITTING THAT THE SENTINELS *ENDED* IT.

AFTER ALL, *THEY'D* BEEN THE ONES TO FINALLY TOUCH IT OFF.

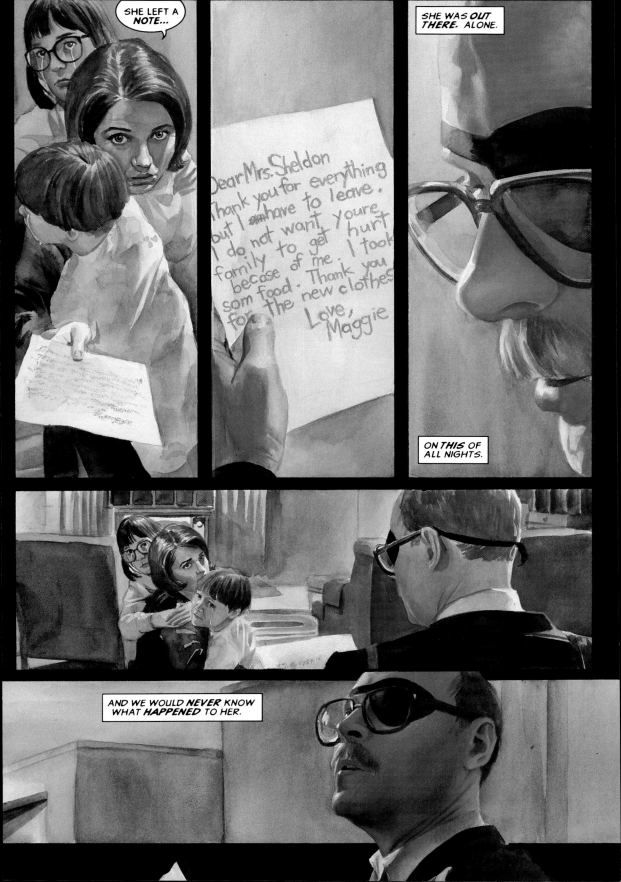

-- SENTINELS HAVE MYSTERIOUSLY *DISAPPEARED,* SOMEWHERE IN THE WESTCHESTER COUNTY AREA.

THE MUTANT TEAM KNOWN AS THE *X-MEN* WERE ALSO SEEN IN THE VICINITY.

AND, OF COURSE I HAD TO WRITE MY ARTICLE ABOUT THE *WEDDING* FOR BARNEY.

NOT HARD NEWS -- CHATTY *ATMOSPHERE* STUFF.

I HAD TO RECAPTURE ALL THAT *MAGIC* AND *JOY,* AND I HAD TO DO IT RIGHT AWAY.

NEWSPAPERS DON'T *WAIT* -- NOT EVEN WEEK-END SUPPLEMENTS.

DADDY?

IS MAGGIE GOING TO BE *ALL RIGHT?*

I --

I --

I WANTED MORE THAN ANYTHING TO TELL HER EVERYTHING WOULD BE *FINE.* THAT THERE WAS A *HAPPY ENDING.*

The third chapter

of **MARVELS** is the one of which I feel most proud. Surprisingly to me, it became my favorite despite the fact that it had never been a part of the original proposal. Before I had even talked to Kurt about it, I conceived **MARVELS'** framework around a loose group of stories starting with the birth of the Human Torch and ending around the death of Gwen Stacy. Observing important events in Marvel history had not been my foremost intention, but as soon as that was determined to be part of our focus, I knew we had to restructure every-

thing and toss out a lot of the short stories I had wanted to tell. But the moment Kurt mentioned the idea of covering the first coming of Galactus (The classic Fantastic Four storyline from issues 48-50) I had a renewed faith in the concept. Luckily, my original idea was underdeveloped enough so that Kurt was able to bring forth what I feel is the greatest moment of the series. The way that Phil Sheldon feels a rising discontent with a city's ungratefulness towards the super heroes that builds to his rage in the last scene, set against the breathtaking events of Judgment Day, hit the spot for me as the most cohesive and driven storytelling that Kurt has ever produced.

For my own part, the way I worked, had gained some momentum by issue 3 and I started to feel like I knew what I was doing (somewhat). Despite the fact that this was the story that was the most exciting to work on, I was affected by a psychological affliction that I shall hereinafter describe as "Kirby Envy". Stan Lee and Jack Kirby's partnership was the best thing that happened to comics in the sixties. Both men were at the top of their form and together gave to this medium what Lennon and McCartney gave to popular music. The Galactus storyline in particular was a highpoint. It remains a landmark in the

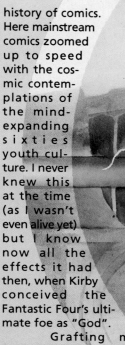

history of comics. Here mainstream comics zoomed up to speed with the cosmic contemplations of the mind-expanding sixties youth culture. I never knew this at the time (as I wasn't even alive yet) but I know now all the effects it had then, when Kirby conceived the Fantastic Four's ultimate foe as "God".

Grafting my style onto classic Kirby images has been one of the most delightful experiences of my life and easily one of the most intimidating. One artist can easily put more polish on another's work by having more time to fuss with it, especially when you're translating traditional pen and ink 4-color art to a more illustrative, painted approach, but to be able to capture the liveliness of Jack Kirby's drawing and the sheer energy of his storytelling is a near-impossible task. I've never cited Kirby as a direct influence on my art or on those artists whom I try to emulate, but that doesn't mean that I'm not mindful of the visual vocabulary he almost single-handedly created for comics.

My first encounter with his work, a short-lived SANDMAN series from the early 70's, struck me as bizarre and expressionistic, but oddly appealing. I soon became aware of his whole evolution through comics history, how he pushed his own boundaries creatively and artistically like no other. Also I encourage those who don't believe that Kirby dabbled in realism to look at FANTAS-TIC FOUR #11 where, in "A Visit With the Fantastic Four," we see realistic rendering come full blown from Kirby in a quiet, almost **MARVELS**-like story about the FF reading their mail.

The time I spent with Kirby's work studying scenes panel by panel to re-interpret sequences, could not have given me a more intimate respect for this man who was a titan in his field. I'm fortunate to have met Jack Kirby a year before his passing and grateful to Kurt Busiek and Marvel Comics for the opportunity to have walked over some of the same ground and enjoyed the beginnings of the universe he was instrumental in creating. This third chapter of **MARVELS** is very honestly intended as an expression of admiration for the single most creative and prolific individual in the history of comics.

God rest you, Jack.

ALEX ROSS

Chapter Three

JUDGMENT DAY

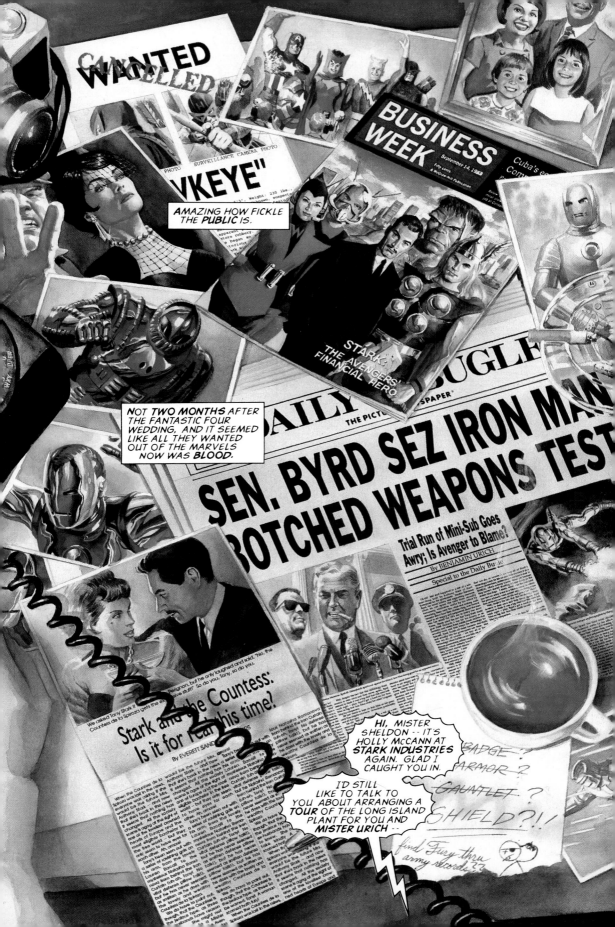

I DON'T THINK THAT'S A *GOOD IDEA*, MISS McCANN.

-- I CAN PROBABLY ARRANGE A PHOTO SHOOT WITH *IRON MAN* HIMSELF, IF THAT WOULD BE --

THANK YOU, MISS McCANN. I'LL HAVE TO GET BACK TO YOU.

THIS IS *DEPRESSING*.

JONAH JAMESON HAD HIRED ME TO WORK WITH BEN URICH, ON A PIECE CALLED, *'IS TONY STARK TRYING TO BUY RESPECT?'*

HE WANTED IT HARD-HITTING. THOROUGH. *UNCOMPROMISING*.

I CAN SEE THE SALES OF MY BOOK *DROPPING* BEFORE MY EYES -- AND I HAVEN'T EVEN *FINISHED* IT YET.

RELAX, PHIL --

-- THE PUBLIC DOESN'T EVEN THINK OF IRON MAN AS *ONE OF* YOUR 'MARVELS.'

HE'S AN *EMPLOYEE*, AN ATHLETE.

HE JUST WEARS THE SUIT -- IT'S NOT LIKE HE *BUILT* IT.

I *GUESS...*

SO WHAT *WAS* TONY STARK UP TO?

BACKING THE AVENGERS -- EMPLOYING IRON MAN --

-- AND HIP-DEEP IN SOME TOP-SECRET GOVERNMENT THING THAT BEN COULDN'T GET WORD ONE ON.

HE WAS BUYING *ATTENTION*, AT LEAST.

UNFORTUNATELY FOR HIM, NOT ALL OF IT WAS GOOD.

BUGLE. URICH HERE.

WHAT?!

UPS-A-DAISY, PHIL! THE AVENGERS'VE BEEN DECLARED A PUBLIC MENACE --

-- WORD IS THE MAYOR'S ABOUT TO ORDER THEM TO DISBAND!

FABULOUS.

I NEED THIS LIKE I NEED A HOLE IN MY HEAD.

IT'S DORIS!

WHICH ONE?

MRS. SHELDON. NOT MRS. URICH.

I'LL TALK TO HER WHEN I GET HOME. TELL HER I'LL BE LATE --

-- AGAIN.

AND NONE OF US -- NOT ONE OF US --

-- SAW IT COMING.

AND WHEN SOMETHING POSITIVE *DID* SURFACE...

-- STRANGE, EGG-SHAPED MENACES SWIFTLY BROUGHT DOWN BY CRACK *S.H.I.E.L.D.* OPERATIVES --

-- ARMED WITH EXPERIMENTAL WEAPONS DESIGNED BY *INDUSTRIALIST TONY STARK* --

WHA-A-AT?!

THE PENTAGON WOULDN'T SAY *BOO* TO ME A WEEK AGO! "SORRY, *NATIONAL SECURITY!*"

BUT STARK'S IN *TROUBLE* NOW -- SO ALL WE HEAR IS *S.H.I.E.L.D.*, *S.H.I.E.L.D.*, *S.H.I.E.L.D.*!

OF ALL THE CALCULATING, *MANIPULA-TIVE* --!

EASY, BEN. WE DON'T KNOW THERE'S A CONNECTION *FOR SURE...*

ALL I WANTED TO DO WAS WRITE THE TEXT FOR MY COLLECTION OF *PHOTOS* --

-- FINISH MY BOOK ON THE MARVELS BEFORE THE *BOTTOM* FELL OUT.

MISTER SHELDON --

MISS McCANN. AGAIN.

I WANTED TO *PERSONALLY* DELIVER THE LATEST PRESS RELEASES FROM THE *IRON MAN FOUNDATION.*

I THINK YOU'LL FIND SOME OF THE *CHARITY WORK* WE DO FASCINATING.

Stark Industries

THE WHOLE THING LEFT A *BAD TASTE* IN MY MOUTH.

IT WASN'T *DEEP*, BUT IT STRETCHED AS FAR AS WE COULD SEE -- !

I'VE GOT TO *GO.*

IT'LL BE WORSE IN THE *LOW-LYING* AREAS -- THERE'LL BE *EVACUATIONS* GOING ON --

NO, PHIL -- !

BUT THE PAPERS -- THEY'LL NEED *PICTURES...*

SO LET *SOMEBODY ELSE* TAKE THEM THIS TIME. YOU PROM- ISED THE GIRLS A *FAMILY* DAY --

-- AND I'M HOLDING YOU *TO* IT!

THIS IS BUT A *SIGN!* THE *END* IS COMING!

THERE SHALL BE *THREE SIGNS,* AND THIS IS THE *FIRST!*

THREE SIGNS AND THEN THE *APOCALYPSE!* THREE SIGNS, AND *JUDGMENT DAY!*

JUDGMENT DAY! I HAVE PROOF!

JERK!

AND I'VE GOT *NOTHING!* WHO WANTS TO BUY PICTURES OF A *DAMP ZOO?!*

IRON MAN AND THE AVENGERS WEREN'T THE ONLY MARVELS GETTING BAD PRESS, EITHER.

FOR A WHILE, IT SEEMED LIKE TROUBLE WAS EVERYWHERE.

SOMEBODY CALL THE *COPS!* SPIDER-MAN *ATTACKED* JONAH JAMESON!

HE'S *RUNNING OFF* -- HE'S SCARED!

HE *CAN'T* BE HUMAN -- AND DO *THAT!*

THIS *PROVES* IT! HE'S A MENACE -- JUST LIKE I'VE ALWAYS *SAID!*

-- MAJOR BATTLE BETWEEN THE *FANTASTIC FOUR* AND A *LARGE, MONSTROUS CREATURE* CAUSED TRAFFIC CONGESTION AND WIDESPREAD *PROPERTY DAMAGE* IN MIDTOWN TODAY --

-- OFF THE STREETS! REPEAT: RETURN TO YOUR HOMES AND STAY OFF THE STREETS!

THE HULK IS ATTACKING THE WHITE HOUSE! SEEK COVER IMMEDIATELY!

THE TIMES

HALF-NAKED SAVAGE CAPTURED ON BRITISH COAST

Daredevil Accused of Murder

PHIL! DINNER!

EAT WITHOUT ME, HONEY -- I'M IN THE MIDDLE OF THINGS HERE!

PHIL...

I'LL BE OUT AS SOON AS I CAN!

MY PHOTOS SHOWED HEROES -- BUT WERE THEY ACCURATE?

ATOMIC POWER HAD BEEN A SHINING MIRACLE ONCE, TOO -- BEFORE THE COLD WAR. BEFORE IT BECAME SOMETHING TO FEAR.

WERE WE MISJUDGING THE MARVELS --

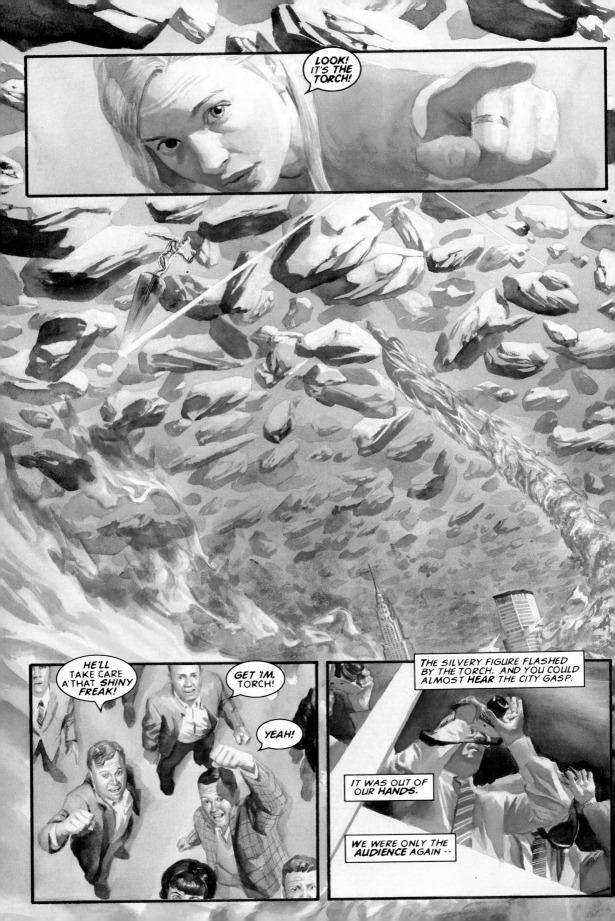

PHIL -- IT'S YOUR *WIFE* --

LATER!

WHY DON'T THE FANTASTIC FOUR COME BACK *OUT?* ARE THEY JUST GOING TO LET THAT GUY KILL US *ALL?*

WHERE ARE THE *AVENGERS?* WHERE *ARE* THEY?!

NOBODY'S *SEEN 'EM!* SPIDER-MAN *NEITHER!*

IT'S ALL OVER...

*O*NCE THE INITIAL *SHOCK* WAS OVER, WE STARTED TO MOVE.

WE WERE *NEWSMEN,* AFTER ALL.

THERE WERE *FACTS* TO BE CHECKED, *REPORTS* TO BE TAKEN DOWN, *COMMUNI-CATIONS* TO BE SET UP.

WE NEEDED CAMERAS IN *POSITION.* EYEWITNESSES. IT WAS *OUR JOB.*

IT WAS SOMETHING TO *DO.*

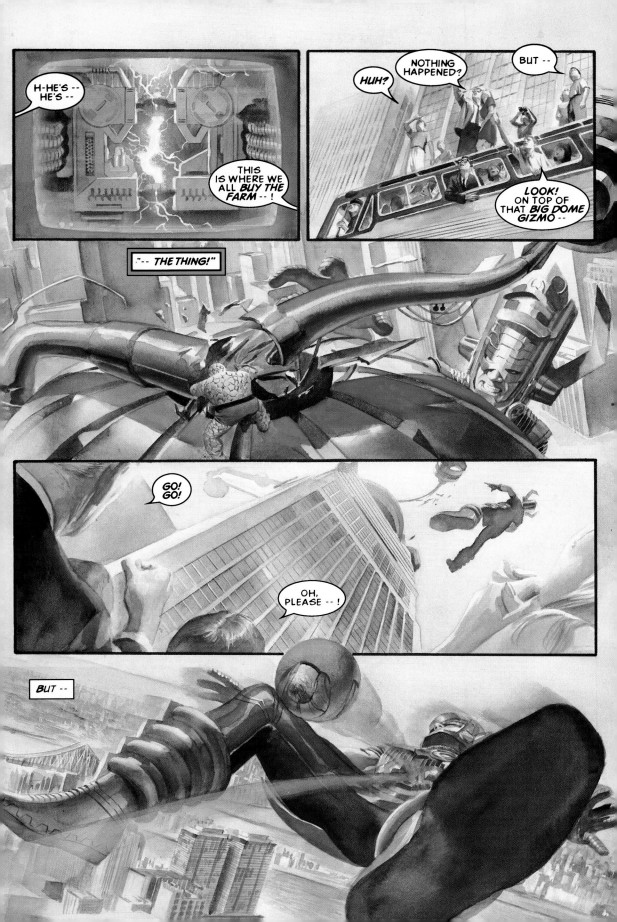

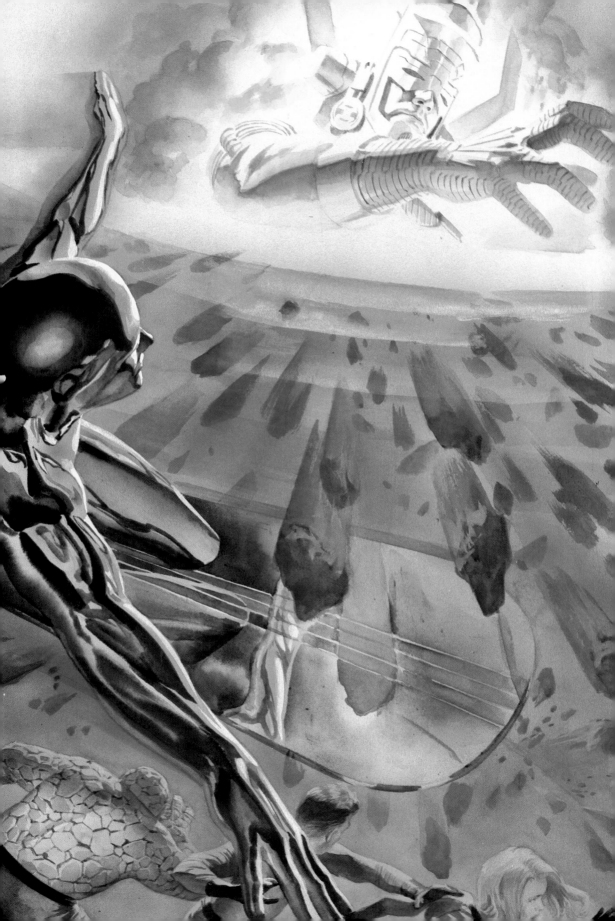

AND THEN --

YOU WOULD HAVE EXPECTED OUR GRATITUDE TO LAST *FOREVER.*

YOU WOULD HAVE EXPECTED US TO *CANONIZE* THE FANTASTIC FOUR --

-- TO RAISE *STATUES* IN THEIR HONOR --

-- NAME *BRIDGES* AND *MOUNTAINS* AFTER THEM AND INVITE THEM TO DINNER AT THE *WHITE HOUSE.*

AT LEAST, *I* WOULD HAVE EXPECTED IT.

SILLY ME.

FINAL ★★★★ **DAILY BUG...**

THE PICTURE NEWSPAPER®

PUBLISHER CALLS GALACTUS HOAX

Editorial by J. Jonah Jameson

EVE...

LA...

...NISHES

...TASTIC FOUR

...AVAILABLE

GOLIATH RETURNS TO THE AVENGERS
Famed Super-Team Trapped Outside City During Crisis

INSTEAD OF TICKER-TAPE PARADES, WE GOT DOUBTS -- ACCUSATIONS -- *INNUENDO.*

WHY HADN'T THEY ACTED *SOONER?*

COULD THEY *PROVE* THE WORLD WAS IN DANGER?

REPORTS CAME IN OF A MOROSE, *SURLY THING,* WANDERING THE BACK ALLEYS OF THE CITY, *FRIGHTENING* PEOPLE.

AND WHO COULD *BLAME* HIM?

BIG THANKS HE GOT.

I CALL 'EM AS I *SEE* 'EM, PHIL -- I ALWAYS HAVE! YOU *KNOW* THAT!

BUT --

MISTER JAMESON!

PARKER! WHAT'VE YOU *GOT* FOR ME?

PICTURES OF SPIDER-MAN FIGHTING THAT *LOOTER* CHARACTER! YOU'LL LOVE 'EM --

-- THEY MAKE OL' SPIDEY LOOK *TERRIBLE!*

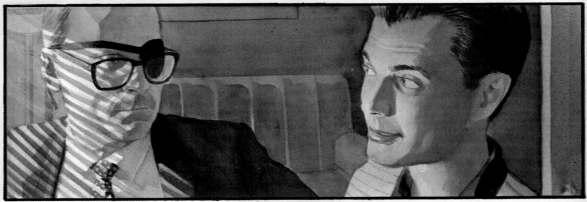

MISTER SHELDON --?

FABULOUS! PERFECT!

NOW *THERE'S* UNBIASED JOURNALISM IN ACTION FOR YOU!

IF *I* WERE SPIDER-MAN, I'D BEAT THE *STUFFING* OUT OF THAT LITTLE WEASEL!

PHIL -- YOU HEAR THE *NEWS?*

OTHER THAN THE FACT THE *OBIT* COLUMN'S A LOT *SHORTER* THAN IT MIGHT HAVE BEEN?

WHAT IS IT?

SENATOR BYRD WENT AHEAD AND *CANCELED* ALL OF STARK'S DEFENSE CONTRACTS.

S.I.'S EXPECTED TO START ANNOUNCING *PLANT CLOSINGS* BY THE END OF THE WEEK.

GOOD! THAT'LL TEACH THAT UPPITY IRON MAN TO *SAVE LIVES* --!

THE WHOLE CITY SEEMED *EMBARRASSED* SOMEHOW -- ASHAMED OF THEIR *TERROR,* NOW THAT IT HAD PASSED AND THEY WERE STILL ALIVE.

AND THEY WERE TAKING IT OUT ON *THE MARVELS,* DENYING WHAT HAD *HAPPENED* --

Commentary by John Romita

We have a special privilege, here around the Marvel offices, of being able to see the artwork in person, before the public has a chance to. As Art Director, I've seen a lot of amazing talent coming from kids (and I use the term loosely) with talent beyond their years. From my first glance at Alex's work, I was impressed. Coupled with the feeling that Kurt put into the events through Phil Sheldon's eyes, we all knew that **MARVELS** would be well received.

As a concept, I feel that the kind of approach that **MARVELS** takes is a dramatic step. I predict that this kind of visual approach of really making the fantastic feel like real life will be used more and more, until "normal" books look weak by comparison. Computer graphics will be an added impetus.

The medium of comics is growing by leaps and bounds, and those who remember the ultimate goal of comics — to tell a story — will always be at the head of the pack. **MARVELS** does that with amazing grace. There have been many milestones in the history of Marvel Comics, and I've been here for a few of them. Now all of you can be here to look back through these pages, and mark a new turning point. You can remember that you were there when **MARVELS** came out.

Looking at this series, I felt like I was looking through a photo album of old friends. In the **MARVELS** series, Alex and Kurt hit all of the important points that I remember in the history of the Marvel Universe. But one event in the final issue touched me especially. That was the death of Gwen Stacy.

There is no great behind-the-scenes drama to tell about that event. Just the usual old tale about the "threatening" mail that came in following it. Mostly the mail was just heartfelt sadness at Gwen's passing. And the recollection that Gerry Conway, the writer at the time, was probably blamed more than he deserved.

My memory of it was a meeting with Gerry, myself, and probably Roy Thomas, in which we discussed giving the readers a "wake-up call" kind of shock that we felt THE AMAZING SPIDER-MAN book could use. I recall Aunt May's death was one option, and I suggested it should be Gwen. That's what we ended up going with. To this day, others, like Stan, think I was wrong. But in the end, it had the effect we wanted. The event was designed to affect readers profoundly, but I was surprised by the quality of Gerry's writing, and still consider it some of the best storytelling, art and writing that I can remember. Gil Kane's pencils were great. It was a turning point of sorts for all comics, and I don't think any character's death has so much affected so many readers since.

Now, Alex and Kurt tell that story from a new viewpoint, without the super hero trappings and fantastic action-adventure, instead pared down to the real human drama of an innocent death. When I was asked to be a part of this by posing for the part of the cabbie who drives Phil after Green Goblin, I loved it. The cameo was lots of fun. I only regret hamming it up so much for the photos.

Still, it is always great being a part of Marvel History. And it was great to see Gwen, one more time.

John Romita

JOHN ROMITA

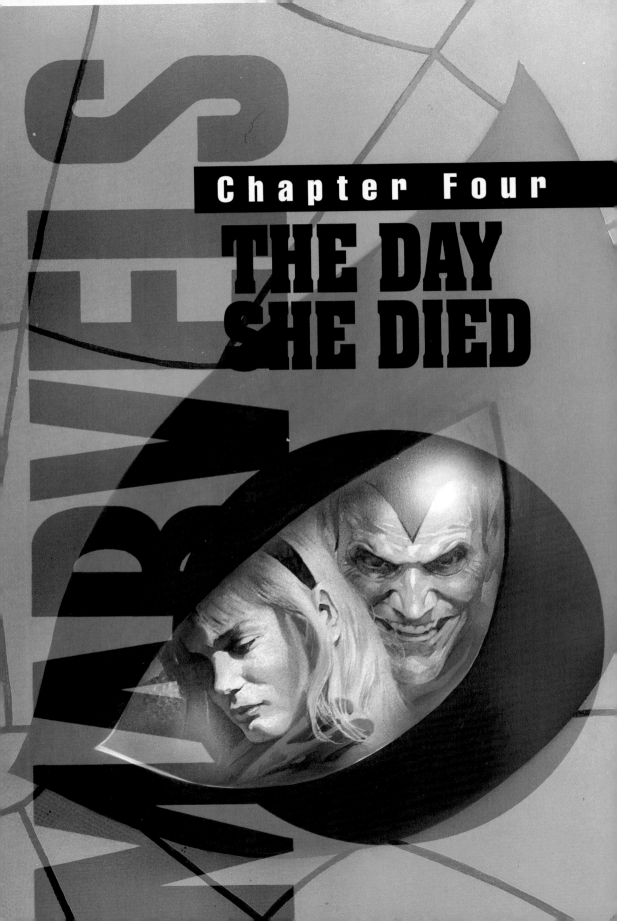

Chapter Four

THE DAY SHE DIED

COULD YOU SIGN IT, "TO MARTIN -- HAPPY FORTY-THIRD BIRTHDAY?"

Book Signing
1:30 - 3:30 TODAY
Meet Photojournalist
Phil Sheldon
Author of
MARVELS
Published by
EMPIRE BOOKS

HOW'S THAT?

THIS IS EXCELLENT, PHIL. FAR BETTER THAN EXPECTED.

I'VE SENT BACK TO THE OFFICE FOR TWO MORE CASES.

WE HAVE TO START TALKING SEQUEL.

MY PUBLISHER WAS DELIGHTED WITH THE SPLASH MY BOOK WAS MAKING, AND I SUPPOSE I SHOULD HAVE BEEN AS WELL.

BUT I KNEW IT WASN'T REALLY MY BOOK THEY WANTED.

I HAD TO TELL YOU -- THIS SHOT OF HAWKEYE --

-- IT'S SO BOLD -- HE LOOKS SO DARING --

THANK YOU. I WAS LUCKY TO GET IT.

THEY WANTED A TALISMAN.

THEY WANTED TO CLAP THEIR HANDS FOR TINKER-BELL AND SAY I BELIEVE, BUT DIDNT KNOW HOW.

THEY WANTED THE AVENGERS TO COME BACK.

ALL WE KNEW WAS THAT THEY WERE IN **ANOTHER GALAXY.**

ALL WE KNEW WAS THAT THEY WERE FIGHTING IN A **WAR** -- A WAR BETWEEN TWO ALIEN RACES. AND IF THEY FAILED, WE WOULD **ALL DIE.**

THERE WERE NO **BULLETINS.** NO **RADIO REPORTS.** HOW **COULD** THERE HAVE BEEN?

ALL WE COULD DO WAS **WAIT.** AND HOPE.

AND, AMID PRAYERS AND CROSSED FINGERS, WE KNEW **ONE THING:**

WE'D **PILLORIED** THEM IN THE STREETS, SLANDERED THEM IN A **SENATE INVESTIGATION** --

OH, WE KNEW NOW WE'D BEEN **WRONG** -- THAT THE SENATOR WHO'D TURNED US AGAINST THEM WAS AN ENEMY ALIEN **HIMSELF** --

UP AGAINST THE WALL AVENGE

THEY WERE LAYING THEIR LIVES ON THE **LINE** FOR US -- AFTER ALL WE'D **DONE** TO THEM.

-- TRIED TO HAVE THEM **FORCIBLY ARRESTED** AS TRAITORS.

-- BUT BY THAT TIME, THEY WERE **GONE.** FIGHTING TO SAVE A WORLD THAT HAD SPIT ON THEM AND **CURSED** THEM.

IN MY DAY, WE'D HAVE BEEN *HONEST* ABOUT IT.

"TONIGHT, *AMERICA* HOLDS HER BREATH AND HOPES THAT *WHEREVER* THEY ARE TONIGHT, HER BOYS ARE *SAFE.*

"WE HANG OUR HEADS AT THE *INJUSTICE* WE HAVE DONE THEM AND SILENTLY BEG THEIR *FORGIVENESS.*"

BUT NOT *TODAY.*

WALTER WINCHELL OR *H.V. KALTENBORN* WOULD HAVE COME ON THE RADIO --

TODAY WE BUY *BOOKS* BY WAY OF APOLOGY AND EYE EACH OTHER IN THE SUBWAY AND SAY *NOTHING.*

AND WHEN THEY *DID* COME BACK AND WE WERE SAFE AGAIN, WE COUGHED AND SAID IT WASN'T *THAT* IMPORTANT ANYWAY.

BAXTER BUILDING

FACE OF A MURDERER
READ THE DAILY BUGLE AND LEARN THE TRUTH!

WE HAD OTHER THINGS TO OCCUPY OUR ATTENTION NOW.

IT WOULD HAVE SERVED US RIGHT IF THEY'D *NEVER* RETURNED.

WE DIDN'T *DESERVE* THEM.

IGGY'S SUPER HEROES

Gloria

WE BAKE OUR OWN BREAD

XTER DING

GATHER 'ROUND, YOU LOSERS AND HAS-BEENS --

-- I'D LIKE TO INTRODUCE *MARCIA HARDESTY*, BIG JACK HARDESTY'S DAUGHTER.

TRY A HOT SUB!

HOT SUB!

SHE'S *JUST HIRED* ON AS MY *ASSISTANT*.

IT'S *NICE* TO *MEET* YOU ALL.

WHAT'S THE *MATTER*, PHIL? TOO *GOOD* FOR US NOW?

IT'S MUNCHIN' TIME!

IT WAS THE *BEST SELLER*. WENT STRAIGHT TO HIS HEAD.

GOT NO TIME FOR WORK *NOW*, OUR PHIL -- HE'S GOT TO DO ALL THE *TALK SHOWS*.

I MIGHT'VE KNOWN. YOU'RE *JACKALS*, ALL OF YOU -- STRIKING AT ANY SIGN OF *WEAKNESS!*

BUT I'M TOO *STUBBORN* TO QUIT AND YOU KNOW IT! DORIS *STILL* HAS TO BADGER ME FOR MONTHS TO TAKE A VACATION.

BUT I'M GETTING OLD. I'M NOT AS *FAST* AS I USED TO BE --

THE *FINAL STRAW* CAME WHILE I WAS ON VACATION.

I WAS *DROWSING* -- DREAMING OF *ANGELS AND GIANTS* AND A *CALM, COMFORTING VOICE* THAT *GLOWED* WITHIN MY HEAD --

PHIL!

PHIL, DID YOU *HEAR* IT?!

WHAT -- ?

IT WAS *GALACTUS!* HE WAS IN *NEW YORK!*

HE RETURNED TO EARTH AGAIN, BUT THE *FANTASTIC FOUR* DROVE HIM OFF!

AND REED RICHARDS --

-- REED RICHARDS *SPOKE* TO EVERYONE SOMEHOW -- RIGHT INTO OUR *MINDS* --

-- *TELLING* US WE WERE *SAFE AGAIN* -- THAT EVERYTHING WAS *ALL RIGHT!*

HE SPOKE *RIGHT INTO OUR MINDS!*

REED RICHARDS, HUH?

YOU MEAN *THIS* REED RICHARDS?

LANDLORD WANTS FANTASTIC FOUR O-U-T!

Eviction Threat Just Latest of Woes for Famous Quartet

I HAD TO **DO** SOMETHING. I DIDN'T KNOW WHAT, BUT --

-- THEY SAVE US AND THEY SAVE US AND WE **INSULT** AND **BELITTLE** THEM.

WE'RE JUST BLIND TO THE TRUTH ABOUT THEM.

DOESN'T THAT SEEM ODD TO YOU?

ly Globe

TNIK!

NOPE. I THINK YOU'VE BEEN THINKING ABOUT THIS **WAAAY** TOO MUCH, PHIL.

YOU'VE WORKED SO **HARD** TO MAKE SURE WE'LL BE ALL RIGHT WHEN YOU RETIRE, PHIL. AND THE BOOK'S BEEN A REAL **WINDFALL.**

I WAS HOPING WE COULD START THINKING ABOUT **FLORIDA...**

I DON'T **KNOW**, MISTER S. I THINK THEY'RE GREAT, AND THEY **DO** GET DUMPED ON A LOT, ESPECIALLY IN THE BUGLE, BUT THIS --

-- THIS SOUNDS KIND OF **RELIGIOUS**, YOU KNOW?

-- BUT I HAD TO DO **SOMETHING.**

I COULDN'T JUST BURY MY HEAD IN THE SAND LIKE EVERYONE ELSE AND PRETEND IT WAS **OKAY** TO --

SPIDER-MAN!

-- STARTLED ME --

-- WHY CAN'T THE POLICE --

-- SO CREEPY --

-- MUR-DERER --

-- JAMESON'S RIGHT --

-- AWFUL --

THAT'S WHEN I REALIZED WHAT I WAS GOING TO DO. I DIDN'T KNOW HOW -- BUT I KNEW WHAT.

I WAS GOING TO BALANCE THE SCALES A LITTLE.

I WAS GOING TO CLEAR SPIDER-MAN OF THE MURDER OF GEORGE STACY.

PHIL!

I'VE GOT AN ASSIGNMENT FOR YOU, IF YOU'VE GOT THE TIME.

SURE, ROBBIE. WHAT'S UP?

PHIL, IF HE *WAS* A HERO -- IF YOUR "MARVELS" WERE *TRULY* THE *NOBLE, SELFLESS CRUSADERS* THEY CLAIM --

-- *HOW* COULD THE *REST* OF US *MEASURE UP?* HOW COULD WE MEET THAT *STANDARD?*

BUT *JONAH* -- WHAT DOES THAT HAVE TO *DO* --

NOTHING! IT HAS *NOTHING* TO DO WITH THE *CASE!*

SPIDER-MAN IS A *GLORY-SEEKING FRAUD* -- AND I'LL EXPOSE HIS *HYPOCRISY* WHENEVER I --

SIR! IT'S COMING IN OVER THE *TELETYPE* --

-- THE *AVENGERS* HAVE BEEN SIGHTED IN *AUSTRALIA!* IT HAS SOMETHING TO DO WITH THE *SENTINELS* --

-- AND THOSE THINGS FROM THE *SUN!*

WE'LL HAVE TO CONTINUE THIS CONVERSATION *LATER,* PHIL. I'VE GOT A PAPER TO RUN.

WAS *THAT* WHAT IT WAS? *JEALOUSY?* WE WERE SO AWED BY THE MARVELS THAT WE HAD TO *GRIND THEM DOWN* --

-- TURN THEM INTO SOMETHING WE COULD *HIRE* AND *FIRE* AT WILL? *WORLDS* SAVED HERE -- TWO CHAIRS, NO WAITING?

IF THAT'S THE CASE, CAGE, YOU'D BETTER *LOOK OUT* --

-- BECAUSE NO MATTER *HOW* LOW A PROFILE YOU KEEP, IT WON'T BE *LOW ENOUGH* --

-- AND ONCE WE'RE THROUGH WITH THE *OTHERS,* WE'LL HAMMER *YOU* DOWN, TOO.

I DON'T KNOW, BARNEY -- I'M SORT OF *WORKING* ON SOMETHING --

PHIL, *PHIL!* EVER SINCE THAT GIANT-MAN SHOT, YOU'RE MY *GOOD LUCK CHARM!* YOU'VE GOT TO DO IT!

YOU DO THIS FOR ME, WE COULD TALK *COLUMN.*

THREE A *WEEK* -- YOUR THOUGHTS ON THE MARVELS, WITH YOUR *PHOTOS* OF COURSE --

LET ME *THINK* ABOUT THAT, BARNEY...

A COLUMN.

MAYBE THAT WOULD BE THE WAY TO DO IT -- TO COUNTER JONAH'S DISTORTIONS ON AN *ONGOING BASIS.*

I MEANT TO TELL BARNEY YES --

-- BUT --

IT'S SET UP, PHIL. I CAN GET YOU IN FOR AN HOUR *THIS* AFTERNOON.

THIS AFTER-NOON? I'M DUE AT SHEA IN HALF AN --

IT'S THE ONLY TIME AVAILA --

FINE. I'LL *BE* THERE.

THIS IS FOR THE *NEW BOOK,* RIGHT?

MAYBE A COLLEC-TION OF *SUPER-VILLAIN* PICTURES? I TRIED THE IDEA ON SALES -- THEY LOVED IT.

WHO DO I *TALK* TO, MISTER SCHWED?

MARCIA!

I CAN'T MAKE THE *THING-THUNDRA* FIGHT!

WHAT? BUT --

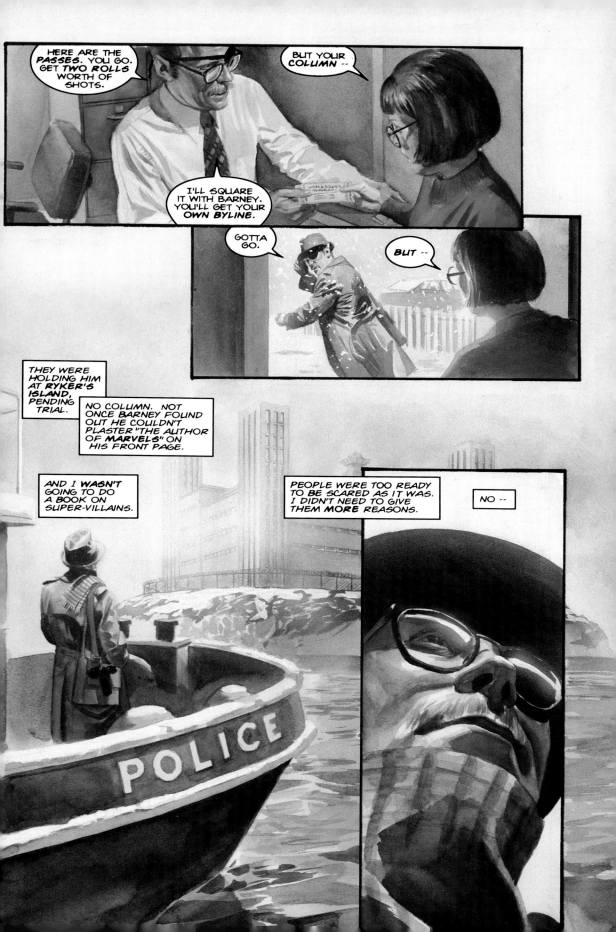

I'D BEEN AFRAID SHE MIGHT NOT AGREE TO TALK TO ME. THE WHOLE SUBJECT MUST HAVE BEEN SO UPSETTING TO HER.

BUT SHE COULDN'T HAVE BEEN MORE FORTHCOMING.

WE TALKED FOR HOURS.

MY FATHER WAS A STERN MAN. HE HAD OLD-FASHIONED VALUES.

BUT YOU COULD TELL -- EVERYTHING HE DID CAME FROM THE HEART --

-- AND YOU COULDN'T BE IN THE SAME ROOM WITH HIM --

-- AND NOT FEEL SAFE.

IT WASN'T UNTIL THE THIRD VISIT THAT WE TALKED ABOUT THE DAY ITSELF.

THEY SAY HE SAVED A BOY -- SAVED HIS LIFE.

HE DIED DOING GOOD. THAT'S MY DAD FOR YOU.

SPIDER-MAN.

I HATE HOW HE SKITTERS. YOU LOOK UP AND THERE HE IS, ALL -- CROUCHED.

I WONDER SOMETIMES IF THERE IS A FACE BEHIND THAT MASK.

I HATED HIM AT FIRST. I KNEW IT WAS HIS FAULT.

BUT NOW I'M NOT SO SURE...

BOY! SOMETHING SMELLS *GREAT* IN HERE!

YOUR HAIR LOOKS *TERRIFIC*, DORIS! ARE YOU DOING SOMETHING NEW WITH IT?

NO, I --

MARCIA! TOMORROW I WANT YOU TO START GOING THROUGH THE *FILES* -- PICKING OUT THE IMAGES YOU THINK ARE MOST *STRIKING*.

GOT TO GET THAT *NEW BOOK* STARTED!

SHE DIDN'T THINK SPIDER-MAN *DID* IT.

SHE DIDN'T *BLAME* HIM. NOT ANYMORE.

YOUR *FATHER DISAGREED* WITH JAMESON?

OH, *VEHEMENTLY.* HE THOUGHT SPIDER-MAN WAS A GOOD MAN. A *HERO.*

THEY'D ARGUE *CONSTANTLY* --

-- CREA- TURES --

-- DO SOME- THING --

-- POLICE, WHERE ARE --

HUH?

-- THEY'LL KILL US *ALL* --

-- OUTTA MY *WAY* --

WHAT'S --

-- oh.

THE **SUB-MARINER** HAD INVA-
DED THE CITY -- TO RECLAIM
AN ATLANTEAN CITIZEN TAKEN
PRISONER BY THE **U.N.**, AS
IT TURNED OUT.

IT WAS RELATIVELY PEACEFUL
AND DIDN'T LAST LONG. NO
DEATHS. SOME PROPERTY
DAMAGE, FOR WHICH NAMOR
MADE *FULL RESTITUTION.*

OF COURSE,
WE DIDN'T
KNOW THAT
AT THE TIME.

THEY
DON'T SEEM TO
BE *HURTING*
ANYONE...

IT'S --

-- AND I SAW NAMOR --

-- BUT I DIDN'T JUST SEE NAMOR AS HE *WAS* --

-- I SAW HIM SINCE THE VERY *BEGINNING* --

-- AND I REMEMBERED HOW EVEN *THEN* WE WERE SO SCARED, WE HOUNDED HIM UNTIL HE LASHED OUT AT US --

-- AND THEN WE LABELED HIM A *VILLAIN* --

-- AND IT FELL INTO PLACE SO NEATLY. THIS WASN'T AN ARTICLE OR A COLUMN OR *ANYTHING* THAT SMALL.

IT WAS MY *BOOK.* MY *NEW* BOOK.

NOT A *PHOTO* BOOK, NOT MORE OF THE SAME, BUT A *REAL* BOOK.

A *MAJOR WORK* ON THE MARVELS AND WHAT THEY SHOULD MEAN TO US.

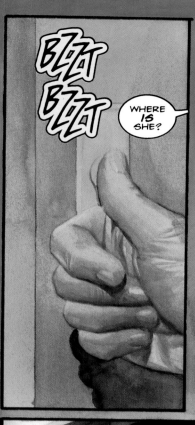

BZZT BZZT

WHERE **IS** SHE?

SHE SAID SHE'D LOOK FOR THE JOURNALS -- SAID SHE DIDN'T KNOW WHERE SHE'D BE --

-- EITHER AT HER PLACE OR HER **BOYFRIEND'S** --

-- I NEVER DID UNDERSTAND WHAT SHE SAW IN THAT WEASEL **PARKER** -- LEECHING OFF SPIDER-MAN'S DEEDS TO EARN A DIRTY **BUCK** --

oh, dear lord.

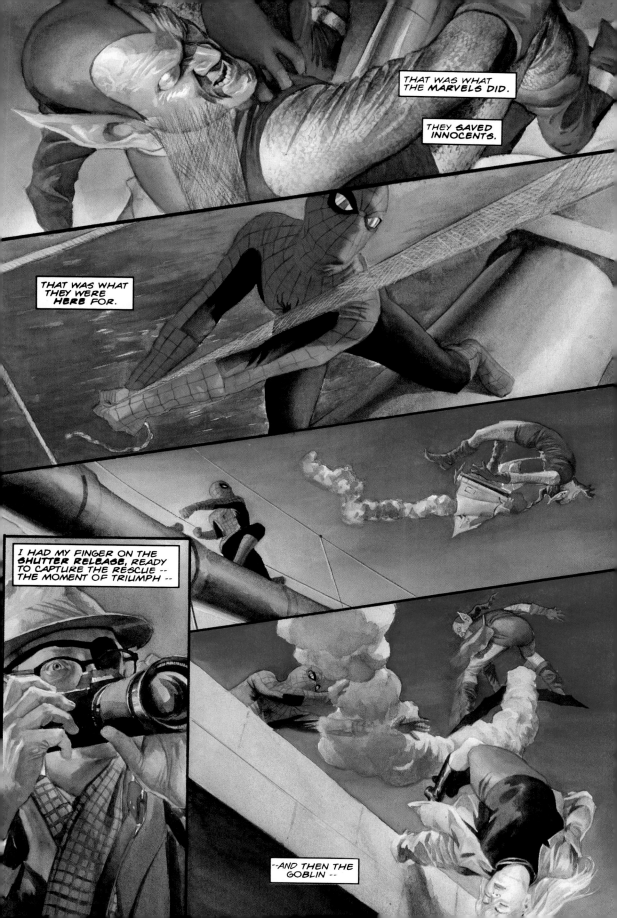

THE REST OF IT WAS A **BLUR**.

THE POLICE --

-- THE OTHER REPORTERS --

-- THE AMBULANCE --

--AND SHE WAS STILL DEAD.

I SWEAR I COULD STILL HEAR THAT *FLAT CRACK*, ECHOING ACROSS THE WATER, ECHOING IN MY EARS.

I READ LATER THAT IT WAS THE SHOCK OF THE *FALL* THAT KILLED HER, BUT IT SURE LOOKED LIKE --

-- IT LOOKED LIKE --

IT DIDN'T *MATTER.* SHE WAS STILL DEAD.

THEY HADN'T *SAVED* HER.

I DON'T *UNDERSTAND!* ALL THE THINGS YOU'VE DONE -- ALL THIS --

-- AND IT'S LIKE IT MEANS *NOTHING* TO YOU!

THERE'S SO MUCH *MORE* YOU COULD DO --

-- MAYBE A FILM ON THE MARVELS -- A *DOCUMENTARY* -- THINGS LIKE THAT DAREDEVIL FOOT-AGE WE SAW --

-- GET ACROSS THE IMPACT OF *SEEING* THEM IN ACTION --

IT JUST WENT ON.

LIKE SHE'D NEVER EXISTED AT ALL. LIKE HER DEATH MEANT NOTHING.

-- HULK AND THE EX-AVENGER CALLED HAWKEYE BATTLED A MONSTROUS ELECTRICAL CREATURE IN LOWER MANHATTAN TODAY.

IT JUST WENT ON.

-- THE BATTLE REACHED THE WATERFRONT, WHERE --

YOU -- YOU CAN STILL *SEE* IT, CAN'T YOU? THIS *DOCUMENTARY* THING -- YOU COULD MAKE IT.

ME? I COULDN'T --

HERE. *TAKE* IT.

WHAT? BUT --

YOU'VE GOT TO BE *OUTSIDE* IT, TO SEE IT FOR WHAT IT IS.

OUTSIDE *WHAT?*

ANYTHING.

EVERYTHING.

WHATEVER. IT'S THE ONLY WAY TO *SEE IT* RIGHT.

YOU'VE GOT TO HAVE THE *EYE* FOR IT, AND MINE IS *GONE.*

I LOST IT SOMEWHERE. I'VE SEEN *TOO MUCH,* AND I'M INSIDE NOW. WHERE I CAN'T SEE ANYTHING STRAIGHT.

BUT YOU -- YOU'RE *YOUNG.* YOU'RE NOT *TIRED.* YOU CAN SEE WHAT I MISS.

MAKE YOUR DOCUMENTARY, MARCIA. ME, I'VE HAD A *GOOD LONG RUN,* BUT IT'S *OVER.*

NO MORE MARVELS FOR ME.

TIME TO *RETIRE.*

Long Island

ANT-MAN AND WASP ALIVE
Dramatic Capture at Avengers
Mansion Marks Heroes' Return

Scott McCloud

Kurt and I had a deal. Kurt and I went to junior high school together back in Lexington, Massachusetts where we both grew up. The deal was that Kurt would come over to my house after school and he would play a game of chess with me (something I was obsessed with at the time) and, in exchange, I would play a game of pool with Kurt on our basement pool table.

Kurt and I had a lot in common. We both liked science fiction, weird British comedy, role-playing games... We were both nerds, basically. Still, there was one thing we did *not* have in common: comic books. Kurt loved comic books but I couldn't stand the things. It took him a while, but Kurt eventually force-fed me enough good back issues that I not only renounced my low opinion of comics, I decided that I wanted to draw them. Lucky for Kurt, since he wanted to be a writer.

Together we produced *The Battle of Lexington,* in which ten Marvel super heroes beat the crap out of each other and destroyed our high school, town library and several historic landmarks in 60 pages of lovingly rendered pencil artwork. Alex Ross, I wasn't, and never could be, but Kurt and I made it feel as realistic as we could.

That was the point after all: to make it *REAL.*

Kurt and I had another deal. Within two years of graduating college, we were both working comics professionals, but somehow we had drifted about as far apart as two people can drift in the comics world. Kurt was deep in the heart of mainstream super hero comics, working to change comics within the "system" as it were. I was off in the independents with my creator-owned series, trying to change comics from the outside. I was getting good reviews, but couldn't sell a comic to save my life. Kurt was writing popular titles, but being ignored by the critics.

So Kurt suggested the deal. I could get all the good reviews, the awards, lecture at the Smithsonian, whatever, but I could never have anything of mine become insanely popular. Kurt, on the other hand, could write the insanely popular series, become filthy rich, but he could never win any awards or get good reviews or anything — that was *my* turf.

And that's just how it turned out in the end. My latest book, UNDERSTANDING COMICS was a big hit with the critics. It won three Harvey Awards, an Eisner Award, all that good stuff. I got all the ego gratification I could ask for. It sold well, sure, but it wasn't *insanely* popular, so I held up my end of the bargain.

Meanwhile, **MARVELS** *is* insanely popular. Everybody loves **MARVELS.** Even black-and-white small press guys like me loved the book. Kurt and Alex's masterpiece sold out in unbelievable quantities for such a high ticket item. Now Kurt gets to sit back and relax as **MARVELS** racks up all the honors he could ever have hoped for: blockbuster sales, great reviews, three Harvey awards, three Eisner aw...

Hey, wait a minute.

Busiek, you cheater!!

SCOTT McCLOUD

"I wear the chain I forged in life"

—Charles Dickens, *A Christmas Carol*

Being shackled to your drawing board is pretty much the status quo for comic book freelancers and MARVELS provided me with that complete deprivation from freedom as well. My enjoyment in working on the series was easily balanced by my exasperation with not being able to do anything *but* work on the series. These 180 pages of story took over a year to complete, with four months spent on each issue and relatively no days off. The extensive research and referencing I did was a large pain, but it was also the thing that kept my interest in the project consistently strong. Over-thinking how to translate these characters and stories visually and trying to figure out how they might actually work made this series come alive for me. I would consider how much pre-production thought goes into big budget films of this genre, and try to put in as much of that attention myself. With comics you have an unlimited budget and you can use as many special effects, props, and actors as you want. Using my friends as models, along with various period references of places, objects, and people, was a way for me to have a stronger identification with the subject matter. My hope was to give the material a life that the reader could be as absorbed by as I was.

A slight alteration easily transformed Mark Braun into either an older or younger Phil Sheldon. ⊃

Overthinking Things

Showing a realistic Human Torch was my first inspiration for MARVELS. After shooting my model in extreme contrast, I took the negative out to study how light might appear to be coming from within a body. I also set a lot of stuff on fire and photographed that, too, till I fully understood the process (and had burned most of my belongings). ∩

Having someone around who understood period clothing from firsthand experience made a big difference. My mother was a fashion illustrator of that era, and she helped design Doris's wedding dress.⊃

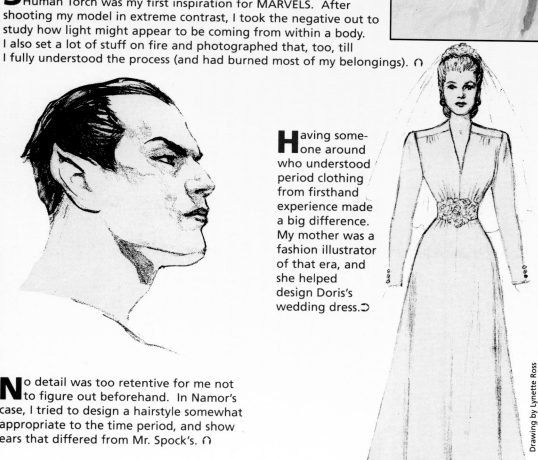

No detail was too retentive for me not to figure out beforehand. In Namor's case, I tried to design a hairstyle somewhat appropriate to the time period, and show ears that differed from Mr. Spock's. ∩

Drawing by Lynette Ross

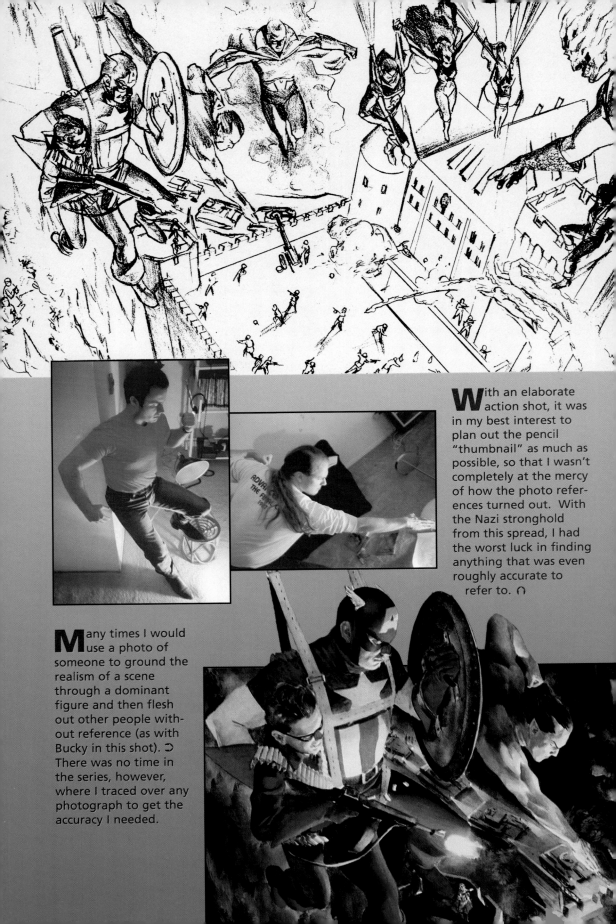

With an elaborate action shot, it was in my best interest to plan out the pencil "thumbnail" as much as possible, so that I wasn't completely at the mercy of how the photo references turned out. With the Nazi stronghold from this spread, I had the worst luck in finding anything that was even roughly accurate to refer to. ∩

Many times I would use a photo of someone to ground the realism of a scene through a dominant figure and then flesh out other people without reference (as with Bucky in this shot). ⊃ There was no time in the series, however, where I traced over any photograph to get the accuracy I needed.

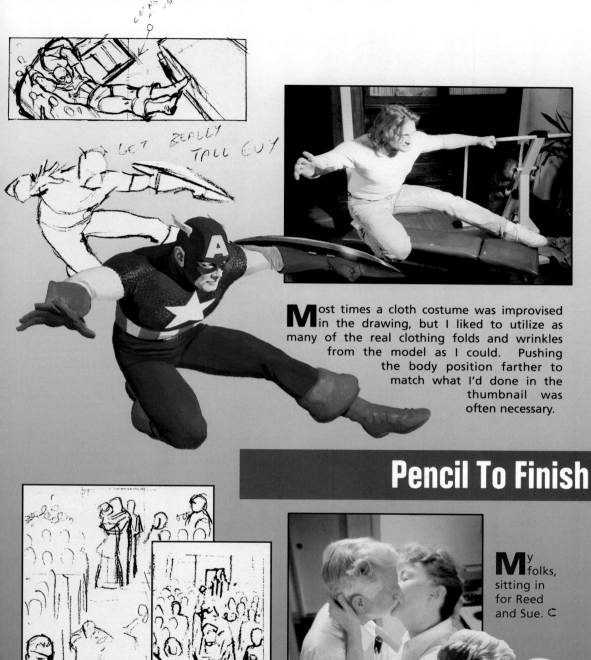

GET REALLY TALL GUY

Most times a cloth costume was improvised in the drawing, but I liked to utilize as many of the real clothing folds and wrinkles from the model as I could. Pushing the body position farther to match what I'd done in the thumbnail was often necessary.

Pencil To Finish

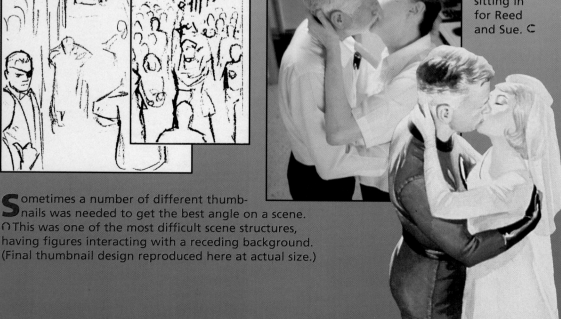

My folks, sitting in for Reed and Sue. ⊂

Sometimes a number of different thumbnails was needed to get the best angle on a scene. ∩ This was one of the most difficult scene structures, having figures interacting with a receding background. (Final thumbnail design reproduced here at actual size.)

Every cover of this series called for a great deal of preparation in design, but few received more response than this one. I thought that I would be asking for a lot to have our big "X-Men issue" adorned with a single logo-riding X-Man from the original series. Luckily my editor and I saw eye-to-eye and it was a short step to the finished design.

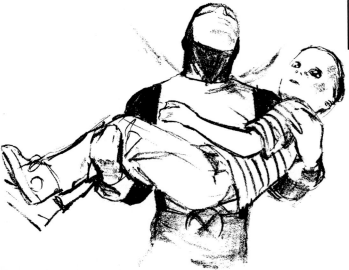

Kurt originally planned the mutant child to be a boy whose obvious mutant quality was that he was green. I had, in the back of my mind, an old Wally Wood EC comic from the fifties that had a frighteningly deformed little girl in it, and I proposed that the boy have something like that appearance to contrast with the more attractive mutation of the Angel. When I sent my design along with a page from the Wood story, Kurt liked the idea well enough to make the character a girl as well.

Wally Wood art from "The Loathsome."

With the layout done (and the kid's gender determined) I could proceed to a color rough. This isn't a step I use often, but here I was unsure about how things would balance color wise, so the thing to do was a tight marker rendition. ∩

For the next step I photographed the main figures. I usually stay away from toys and model kits since they can be too stiff to achieve the poses, but in this case a couple of dolls did the job perfectly. After the final pencil was done it took about a day or two to finish the painting. ∩

Some touch-up with airbrush is used for the sky and angel's wings but mostly the medium was watercolor and gouache paints worked both transparent and opaque. ⊃

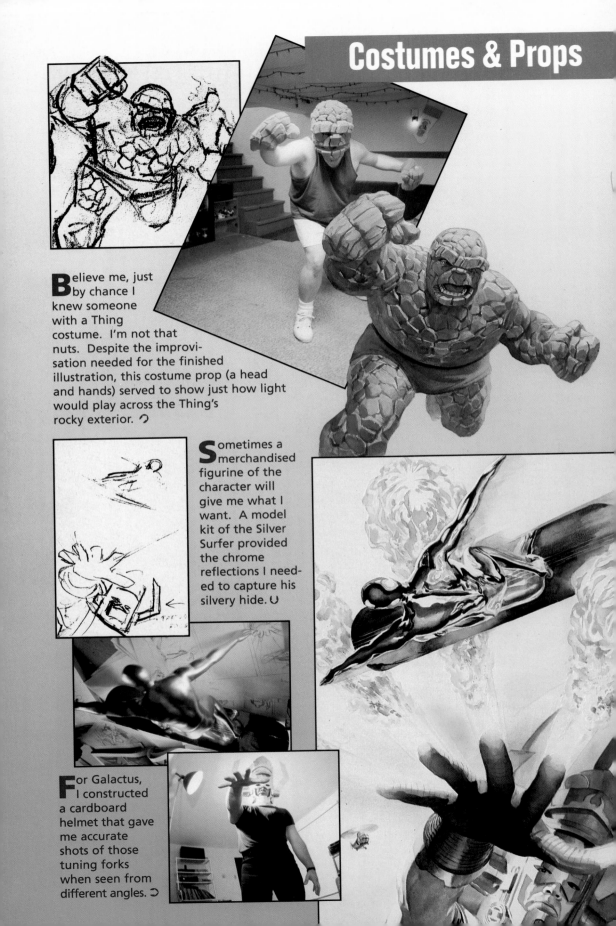

Believe me, just by chance I knew someone with a Thing costume. I'm not that nuts. Despite the improvisation needed for the finished illustration, this costume prop (a head and hands) served to show just how light would play across the Thing's rocky exterior. ↻

Sometimes a merchandised figurine of the character will give me what I want. A model kit of the Silver Surfer provided the chrome reflections I needed to capture his silvery hide. ↺

For Galactus, I constructed a cardboard helmet that gave me accurate shots of those tuning forks when seen from different angles. ↻

Models

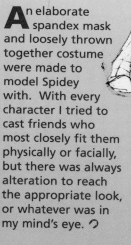

An elaborate spandex mask and loosely thrown together costume were made to model Spidey with. With every character I tried to cast friends who most closely fit them physically or facially, but there was always alteration to reach the appropriate look, or whatever was in my mind's eye. ↷

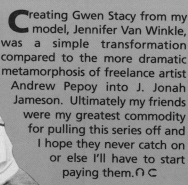

Creating Gwen Stacy from my model, Jennifer Van Winkle, was a simple transformation compared to the more dramatic metamorphosis of freelance artist Andrew Pepoy into J. Jonah Jameson. Ultimately my friends were my greatest commodity for pulling this series off and I hope they never catch on or else I'll have to start paying them. ↶ ⊂

Acknowledgements

Kurt Busiek

I'd like to thank Jeff Gelb, Andrew Pepoy and Karl Kesel for graciously loaning me reference material from their collections, and my amazingly tolerant wife, Ann, along with Richard Howell, James W. Fry III and Scott and Ivy McCloud, for their support, friendship and encouragement during the conception and writing of **MARVELS**.

Alex and I would also like to dedicate the entire work, with respect, admiration and gratitude, to the memory and the achievements of Jack Kirby.

Alex Ross

As much as I can't bear to admit it, this project would not have been possible without a "few" other people pitching in with their time to pose for me, and I owe a great debt of gratitude to all of them. Firstly, I'd like to thank my folks, Clark & Lynette, for modeling and for serving as inspiration as they have lived through every age that the series takes place in. My thanks goes to:

FRANK KASY The Human Torch, Captain America, Thor, Giant Man, Iron Man

JIM WISNEWSKI Phineas Horton, Otto Octavius

ANDREW PEPOY J. Jonah Jameson

LAURIE JOHNSON Doris Jacquet

MARK KOLODNY Iggy

MATT PAOLETTI Captain America, Nick Fury, Galactus, Goliath, Iron Man, Captain Marvel, Thor, and countless others

STEVE DARNALL Fred

RON BOGACKI Casey, Barney Bushkin, the Thing

DEL CLOSE Bennett Schwed

BARRY CRAIN Cyclops, Mister Fantastic

HOLLY BLESSEN Invisible Girl

JANE JENSEN Marvel Girl

JIM MARCUS Beast

ELIZABETH BRAUN Jenny

LAURA BRAUN Beth, Maggie

JULIE WALE Patsy Walker, Betty Brant

MARK HUCKLEBONE Johnny Storm

MIKE SPOONER Ben Urich

JON OYE Peter Parker

LISA BEADERSTADT Marcia Hardesty

TONY AKINS Joe Robertson, Luke Cage

JENNIFER VAN WINKLE Gwen Stacy

KEN KOOL Spider-Man

JONATHAN KASY
MEG GUTTMAN
BOB MILLER
JULIE FREEDMAN
MARY BRAUN
LENIN DEL SOL

SUE NIGGEMAN
BRIAN AZZARELLO
RICK THERRIO
HILARY BARTA
NORM DWYER
MIKE SAENZ
KURT AND ANN BUSIEK

LINDSAY ROSS
STEVEN STRAUCH
BRIAN COBERLY
SUNG KOO
SCOTT BEADERSTADT
JOHN ROMITA, SR.

and most of all, **MARK BRAUN**, who gave so generously of his time and patience to play Phil.